T0129070

True Love

True Love

Wait! What Is True Love?

PRISCILLA ALAN

ARCHWAY
PUBLISHING

Copyright © 2018 Priscilla Alan.

All rights reserved. No part of this book may be used or reproduced by
any means, graphic, electronic, or mechanical, including photocopying,
recording, taping or by any information storage retrieval system
without the written permission of the author except in the case of
brief quotations embodied in critical articles and reviews.

This book is a work of non-fiction. Unless otherwise noted, the author
and the publisher make no explicit guarantees as to the accuracy of
the information contained in this book and in some cases, names of
people and places have been altered to protect their privacy.

Scripture taken from the King James Version of the Bible.

THE HOLY BIBLE, NEW INTERNATIONAL VERSION®,
NIV® Copyright © 1973, 1978, 1984, 2011 by Biblica, Inc.®
Used by permission. All rights reserved worldwide.

Archway Publishing books may be ordered through booksellers or by contacting:

Archway Publishing
1663 Liberty Drive
Bloomington, IN 47403
www.archwaypublishing.com
1 (888) 242-5904

Because of the dynamic nature of the Internet, any web addresses or
links contained in this book may have changed since publication and
may no longer be valid. The views expressed in this work are solely those
of the author and do not necessarily reflect the views of the publisher,
and the publisher hereby disclaims any responsibility for them.

Any people depicted in stock imagery provided by Thinkstock are models,
and such images are being used for illustrative purposes only.
Certain stock imagery © Thinkstock.

ISBN: 978-1-4808-5687-5 (sc)
ISBN: 978-1-4808-5688-2 (e)

Library of Congress Control Number: 2018900264

Print information available on the last page.

Archway Publishing rev. date: 1/11/2018

Contents

1 Corinthians 13

1. If I speak in the tongues of men or of angels, but do not have love, I am only a resounding gong or a clanging cymbal.
2. If I have the gift of prophecy and can fathom all mysteries and all knowledge, and if I have a faith that can move mountains, but do not have love, I am nothing.
3. If I give all I possess to the poor and give over my body to hardship that I may boast, but do not have love, I gain nothing.
4. Love is patient, love is kind. It does not envy, it does not boast, it is not proud.
5. It does not dishonor others, it is not self-seeking, it is not easily angered, it keeps no record of wrongs.
6. Love does not delight in evil but rejoices with the truth.
7. It always protects, always trusts, always hopes, and always perseveres.
8. Love never fails. (Bible, 2016)

Introduction

"When I die, the main thing I want everyone to remember about me is that I truly loved them." I said these words to my therapist about ten years ago in one of my many counseling sessions. It wasn't long after, when this desire was tested beyond anything I could have ever imagined. A family member that I loved, or at least thought I loved, hurt my family in a way that I never dreamed he could. It was at that time I realized my desire of loving everyone I knew was probably an impossibility. I would never truly love him again, nor did I want to.

What is true love anyway? Why is it so important to love and be loved? What good would it do if those I was closest to didn't return my love? Is there even such a thing as true love? I have often wondered if true love exists and if it does, how do I feel it? How do I achieve loving and being truly loved? When asked what true love is, many people give these answers: I don't know what true love is, true love is putting others above yourself, true love brings happiness or contentment, or true love is a choice. In a world where we use the word "love" nearly every day, why don't a lot of us know if there is such a thing as true love or what it is? Why do some people believe in it, yet others never do? I believe, at least in my experience, that we get into our heads an idea of what true love is and then we go searching for it, but when it doesn't meet our expectations, we become disappointed, change our belief of it, and look for it in some other form, only to become disappointed again.

I used to believe true love was that warm, fuzzy feeling you get when you see someone who just makes your heart go all aflutter. Something similar to what you feel when your waitress brings your chocolate brownie, covered in ice cream and whipped topping, to the table. Something like the feeling you get when the finishing touches are done on a task that you've been working on for quite some time. Something between the warm, summer sun and the fresh, new, white snow of winter.

What do I believe true love is now? All the above, and so much more! I have found in life that love is just too much to explain in all the books and chapters in the world. I don't believe any one person has the full answer to this question, but one Man has lived it. I hope to show you on the pages of this book what I believe true love is all about and it's my hope that my story will help you love, and be loved, in a way you never thought possible.

True Love is Patient

In the beginning was the Word, and the Word was with
God, and the Word was God. He was with God in the
beginning. Through Him all things were made; without
Him nothing was made that has been made. In Him was life,
and that life was the light of all mankind. The light shines
in the darkness, and the darkness has not overcome it.
John 1:1-5

Jesus was the Word, come to life, in the flesh, and has been with
God from the beginning of time. He was with God when the
world was created. He was with God when life was first breathed
into Adam and Eve and when sin entered the world. He was with
God when Noah built the Ark and when Moses parted the waters.
He was with God when David fought Goliath and Solomon built
the temple. Jesus was with God from the very start of time, but He
chose to take on flesh, become man, and live here on this Earth to
show us how God wants us to live. But He was rejected and killed
because we did not understand Him and why He was here.

I am just in awe that He would even consider doing this for
us! If I lived in a perfect place, a place of peace and harmony and
joy, there's no way I would leave it to come into a place of chaos
and hurting, confusion and anger; only to be spat upon and beaten
because of a stubborn and unbelieving people. Jesus lived here for

thirty-three years, thirty-three long patient years. If this task were left to me, I would have skipped all the childhood, the teen years, even the messed up young adult age, and jumped right to the end. Just get the cross over with already!

But I am not Jesus and neither is anyone else. Many people talk about the cross and what He did for us there, but in my opinion, what was even more difficult for Him was all those years of never losing His cool and lashing out at people. All those years of being understanding and loving and kind to people who so didn't deserve kindness. Can you imagine when Joseph or Mary were being impatient or selfish, how difficult it would have been for Jesus, after having lived in Heaven all that time, to not have told them to just get over themselves?

But the Bible tells us in 2 Corinthians 5:21 that "God made Him who had no sin to be sin for us, so that in Him we might become the righteousness of God." He was sinless, God made Him sinless, yet He lived those years patiently understanding *our* sinful natures. He never disrespected His parents. He didn't lash out at His siblings when they took the biggest piece of cake or played with his toys without asking. He didn't take a second glance at the teenage girls who gave Him a wink and a smile. He didn't ever drive the horse too fast or sneak out the window to spend an evening on the town with His friends.

Jesus's patience at never having done any of these things just baffles my mind. Yes, the cross would have been terrible, and yes, the cross is one of the most horrific things that I can imagine anyone would ever have had to endure. But for me, being patient all those years so He could accomplish His goal, the goal of remaining sinless so He could be the sacrifice, the perfect sacrifice for our sins, was the true test of His patient love for us. It was the ultimate act of true love, through patience, that anyone could have ever given.

Patience is a virtue I have not been blessed with. Waiting for something has always been a struggle for me. When God handed out patience, I got tired of waiting in line, told someone else they could have my portion, and moved on. Yes, that's me! Not having patience has taught me lesson after lesson in life. The hardest ones have come with the greatest consequences! I have discovered that there are people who will quickly play on your weakness, whether it's a lack of patience like mine, or some other insecurity. I believe allowing these types of people access into your heart will cause the deepest form of pain you can ever know.

From the time I was a small child, my lack of patience has been my downfall. The thing I was most impatient about was wanting to find my true love. I knew he was out there somewhere and I used to daydream about being his wife and raising his children. I watched my parents love and I longed so bad to have someone love me the way they did each other. Their marriage was not perfect, no marriage is. They fought sometimes and life was difficult for them, but I would see them kissing or hugging on occasion, and I couldn't wait till I could find someone to hug and kiss me too. They loved me, at least I hoped and thought they did, but affection wasn't a big thing in our house. The only time we were really hugged or kissed was at night and "I love you" was something that very seldom was ever said.

When I came along, my mother already had three kids. I was the youngest then and she was much too busy for me. I really enjoyed my time with her when the other kids were all in school. I used to stand at the machine to watch as she would sew our Easter dresses or mend our clothes. I would get the cake batter bowl all to myself, or sometimes she had the time to read books to me and only me. I was always happy to see my brother and two sisters when they got home, but then her attention was directed to them so I was on my own again.

My dad was a logger and he and my grandfather would be gone for long hours, and I don't remember seeing him much when I was very little. Sometimes Dad would take us to the woods with him. I loved the smell of the fresh fallen oak trees. I always thought it was so cool to see the water flow from the inside of the trees as he cut them down. The smell of the decaying leaves in the spring was the worst smell in the world to me. Often, I would go set in the truck because I couldn't take that smell for too long without becoming nauseated. Dad would never let us be around much when he was falling the trees, he was always careful to tell us not to ever be downhill from them when they came down. He always made sure we were well out of the way before he began cutting.

Grandpa ran the skidder; he would tie a cable to the end of the log after Dad had all the limbs cleaned up. Then us kids would move the limbs away if they weren't too big. Grandpa would drag the log up to the top of the hill and leave it close to the log truck. Later, after they had enough logs to fill the truck, Dad and Grandpa would load the logs with the caterpillar and tie them down with chains and if it weren't too late in the day, he would haul them to the sawmill. It was a fun day for me to be allowed to go, but again, it was a lonely day because they were working and I spent most of the day setting on a rock or picking wildflowers or looking at a new growth of mushrooms.

When I finally got to go to school, I would see boys and girls interacting as boys and girls do and I wanted so bad for someone to care about me that way. This lack of attention and affection caused me to literally have a crush on almost every boy I knew, and I wasn't shy about letting them know. Except for that red headed boy who I always had to set by in third and fourth grade. I might have liked him if he would have taken a bath and kept his nose wiped. He had a huge crush on me and was not shy about it, but he was not the husband I had envisioned, so I never even gave him a chance.

In the small town I grew up in there were only about 25 kids in my class. Half of those kids were girls and much of the other half I was related to. At family reunions, we could have almost had a school lesson. Eventually, I branched out to other classes when none of the boys in my own class were interested or eligible. I was determined to find my true love, and I wasn't really very picky about who he was or how long I had to look. Waiting on God to find the right boy for me or just being happy to be a little girl was not my heart's desire. Being loved was all I dwelt on most of the time.

This set me up for a lifetime of heartbreak. I went quickly from one crush to another looking for someone to truly love me. I had been in church and knew that I needed to wait on God to send my true love, but I didn't want to wait. Remember, I had no patience, and realizing the patience Jesus had endured for me, so that I may have a way to heaven, has been a very difficult concept to understand. Some days loneliness creeps into my soul and I become irritable and impatient, longing to continue my search for true love, a true love that is already within my grasp.

True Love is Kind

When one of the Pharisees invited Jesus to have dinner with him, He went to the Pharisee's house and reclined at the table. A woman in that town who lived a sinful life learned that Jesus was eating at the Pharisee's house, so she came there with an alabaster jar of perfume. As she stood behind Him at His feet, weeping, she began to wet His feet with her tears. Then she wiped them with her hair, kissed them and poured perfume on them. When the Pharisee who had invited Him saw this, he said to himself, "If this man were a prophet, He would know who is touching Him and what kind of woman she is—that she is a sinner."

Luke 7:36-39

Can't we all just see ourselves in this Pharisee's shoes? We have heard about Jesus and how popular He is, and we want in on that. We want everyone to say that we must be a wonderful person to have Jesus to our house for dinner. I'm sure this Pharisee put on a grand spread for Jesus, and I'm sure he went all out to let everyone know who was coming to his house that evening, just like I am sure we would have. But then when this person came, a dinner crasher we would call her today, uninvited, probably dirty and smelly, and tried to steal his show, the Pharisee had nothing nice to think of her. And not only her, but also Jesus. He thought that Jesus must not be who He said He was if He was just going to let this sinful woman touch Him.

What the Pharisee didn't understand was that Jesus knew exactly who this woman was, and He knew her past and all her history. He knew what she had been through in her life and what her future held. He knew how many men she had been with, and how many times she had been to the temple to sacrifice for her sins. Jesus knew it all! Yet, He sat there and let her do this to Him. Why? Because He was in love with her. Not because she was doing Him any special favors, but simply because she was human. She was a sinner, just like the rest of humanity, just like this Pharisee. And Jesus loved her just as much as He did the Pharisee. He loved her just the same as He loves you and me.

He could have reprimanded her and sent her away ashamed and hurt, but in His kindness, in His love, He allowed her to continue her task. He knew she had this perfume, probably her most prized possession, that she had intended to sell for money someday when times got rough, yet for some reason all she felt was that she needed to give it to Him. I believe she knew He was sent from God, and it was her deepest desire to give Him all she had, and that perfume was it. And Jesus, in His loving kindness, allowed it.

While growing up, our house sat on a dirt road about one mile from my grandparent's house. Walking to their house was a regular-past-time for us; sometimes we would do it more than once a day, and there were many ways to get there from our house. In the woods behind our house, our property connected to my grandparent's property so we could walk along the road path. If we went that way, it usually took longer than normal because we had to stop and play in the creek, or watch the cows, or pick some flowers for Grandma's table. We could also cut through the neighbor's field if they didn't have a mean bull at the time. But the old, dirt, country road was our most often traveled route. It was a pretty easy walk except for the one hill that was a blessing going down, but a curse coming back.

Grandma's house was always a treat for us. There was a continuous supply of cookies in the cookie jar or she had some other kind of yumminess in the oven. She only stood "Four-feet- eleven" (Evie, 1977) inches, but the love my grandmother had for her grandkids could have made her "ten-feet-tall." She was always so happy to see us, and it was hugs and kisses from her each time we went. When we were smaller, she would regularly let us climb onto her lap in the rocking chair to read us a book. There were stairs in her house, and she fixed a little play place under them for us to spend time. She hung pictures and put coloring books and crayons and a little table inside.

Upstairs there was a full porch and we could usually play out there all we wanted to. Grandma had an old trunk full of clothes that we could dress up in. I usually went there first, which is the subject for a poem that she wrote about me. There were old dolls and many days I spent practicing braiding their hair. I would do it over and over until I had each doll ready for an outing. She always had some kind of old makeup for me to wear, and I would put on some shoes, and a dress, and grab an old purse, and me and my dolls would head outside to go shopping. We always found some interesting things: rocks, sticks, walnuts, flowers. I would bring them back inside and lay my treasures out on the kitchen table for Grandma to inspect. She was truly so interested in everything I had found.

Over time my grandmother became my best friend. Sometimes I would call her just to hear her voice. I didn't ever really need to tell her anything in particular; I just wanted to know she was there. As I began to get older and my likes and dislikes changed, she changed with me. Instead of shopping trips, she would send me out to gather the eggs, or to go find a hen that had hatched a new set of chicks. She would have me count them and make sure they were all ok, always with the warning not to get too close.

My grandmother was a great wanderer. Many times when I got there, she was out on a walk somewhere. Sometimes I could find her, but often I would have to wait an hour or longer until she came back in. She knew every flower's name and where they grew. I loved going on a walk with her because it wasn't fast paced in order to lose weight or see how far she could go and how quickly. It was a slow, steady, walk where we stopped every few minutes for a special rock or a patch of moss. She was always bringing some kind of treasure home and adding it to her own flower beds. She would point out to me a special mushroom patch, or we would check for wild strawberries or pick some paw-paws.

Grandma was a part of the local ladies' club. It was a group of women, from the holler where we lived, and from town, who got together once a month to do special things for people.

Of course, there was no gossip exchanged, their sole purpose was to do good. They would put out a new cookbook or make a quilt and each meeting always included a grand potluck meal. One year they made quilts for each of my siblings and me. It was one of the best gifts I had ever received, and I still have my pink and purple quilt some forty years later.

Summertime was my favorite time because my cousins from Oregon would come for a few weeks. We spent every moment together, that we were able, when they were here. Two of them were my age and we got along very well. One day as Mindy and I sat out in our grandparent's front yard, we saw my grandpa's dog, Boomer, setting alone under a tree. I got up to go over and pet him and as I sat down beside him, he growled at me. Mindy immediately warned me that her dad said when a dog growls at you, it meant to stay away.

My dad and grandpa were coon hunters. They spent many fall and winter nights in the woods and usually brought home something for their efforts. My dad had many black-and-tan hound dogs all the time, which is what Boomer was too. He had the dogs spread out all around our yard in their little houses made from hollow tree trunks which my dad would bring home from the woods and attach a top to. I loved every one of those dogs, and made sure they were more than just hunting dogs, they were also pets. My favorite dog was named Squeak. He had been born within just a few months of me and we were growing up together. Dad would not have a mean dog and anytime any of them showed the slightest hint of being aggressive, he would not allow us to get near it and he would get rid of that dog as quick as he could. Boomer had been showing some signs of meanness, but he was Grandpa's dog, and he wanted to keep him around because he was a good guard dog for my grandmother when he was gone.

As Mindy was yelling at me to get away from him, I leaned over and got down close to his face to show her I didn't care that he was growling; I loved him anyway and I knew he loved me. The next moment he had me on the ground under him, barking and growling and biting at my face. I could see Mindy screaming and running to the house. I don't know how it happened, but I was able to position my feet right under his belly and push him off me. At that same time, my grandmother and the others inside came running out. When Boomer saw them, he ran away. I was not hurt bad and had only one good bite on my nose, but my grandmother didn't care. This was the last straw for her and she wanted that dog gone. Grandpa didn't get rid of him, but kept him around a few more years and as he continued to get more and more aggressive, even chasing my grandmother inside a few times, the family became more upset about him too. Then one day, mysteriously, Boomer disappeared.

I was so fortunate to have a grandmother like her. She was a pretty healthy person until I was about fourteen. They got their kitchen water from a spring which fed out of the side of the hill their home sat beside. The water trickled down the hill through a pipe that went directly into the sink. She was doing dishes one day as a storm came in, when lightening hit the spring and went right into the dish-water she had her hands in. It put her in bed for about two weeks. Not long after that one of my cousins had a baby die of meningitis. My grandmother never recovered from those two events and I could feel both the weakness and sadness in her each time I was there after that.

Her health then began to deteriorate. She didn't feel like walking much anymore and the cookie jar was usually empty. She began going to different doctors telling them she had a lump in her side causing pain. They told her it was just a gas bubble and gave her some home remedies to try, but the "bubble" never went away. Finally, one doctor listened to her. Exploratory surgery revealed her internal organs were completely surrounded by the "bubble' of cancer that was quickly spreading. The cancer had begun as skin melanoma on her back and spread. They sent her home and said there was nothing they could do.

It was little more than a month later that I stood by her hospital bed in her living room staring into her eyes and crying because my best friend was leaving me. I was sixteen and my world was falling apart with her departure. She was in a coma, but I felt she knew I was there. I held her hand and told her I loved her and thanked her for loving me so much. She had been my rock during the most tragic times of my life and now she was going home. I said goodbye, knowing this would be the final time. It was about ten o'clock when I went home and crawled into bed, eyes swollen from crying and begging God not to take her from me. Just before dozing off, there she was, hovering over my bed, telling me goodbye. Was it a dream? A few minutes later my sister came into my room and told me that she was gone.

My Grandmothers kindness, not only to me, but to all the other grandkids too, will always live in my heart and I am so grateful to have had her. I love to sit and read her book of poems that tells of her walks and the flowers she encountered and her mushroom patch. She also wrote poems about several of the grandkids. The one about me tells of my shopping adventures with my dolls. I am glad I have those memories of her so I can reminisce of how she was a picture of true love for us. Even though she was not perfect; she hated to clean house and she spent many hours on the phone hearing the latest gossip, she always loved me and my cousins unconditionally. No matter what mistakes we made or how in trouble we had been at home, we always knew her house was a place of safety and love. We always knew she would do whatever she could to show her true loving kindness for us.

True Love does not Envy

For from within, out of men's hearts, come evil thoughts,
sexual immorality, theft, murder, adultery, greed, malice,
deceit, lewdness, envy, slander, arrogance and folly.
Mark 7:21-22

Wow! Jesus sure packed a lot in those two verses. If we look at those words closely we will see we all fit into one of those categories. Let's look at this scripture a little deeper by going back to the beginning of chapter seven. The Pharisees and teachers of the law had come to seek out Jesus and His disciples. When they found them, the Pharisee's became upset that some of them were eating with unclean hands. They asked Jesus why they did not follow the traditions of the elders by ceremonially washing first. "After the Babylonian captivity, the Jewish rabbis began to make meticulous rules and regulations governing the daily life of the people. These were interpretations and applications of the law of Moses, handed down from generation to generation." (Commentary, 1985) This was not a written law, but only one of the many they came up with in order to control the people.

Jesus explained to them it is not what we put into our mouths that makes us unclean, like dirt and germs, but it's what comes from the heart that makes us do and act in a way that makes us sinful. These Pharisees and teachers wanted the people to follow their own rules and laws, and if the people chose not to, then they liked to believe themselves more righteous than everyone else. Jesus often referred to them as hypocrites because their hearts were so dirty inside, even though their outside appearance was clean and well dressed.

The word envy can be defined as "a feeling of discontented or resentful longing aroused by someone else's possessions, qualities, or luck." (Google Dictionary) In this passage of scripture, the Pharisees and teachers were showing envy, because here sat Jesus, someone the people had been saying was sent from God, someone who was Jewish by birth and was required to follow all the Jewish rules, yet He sat eating with people who had not washed their hands before putting food into their mouths. All their lives the Pharisees had been required to wash first, but now Jesus was messing up their traditions.

Jesus messed up many of their beliefs in His time on Earth. I like to explain it to my church kids this way. You have been taught all your life its ok to steal your classmates pencil if they have more than one. When they aren't looking, or if they drop theirs on the floor, you may take it and they can do nothing about it. It's the law, that stealing someone's pencil is allowed when they have plenty. But then Jesus came along and told you it's not ok to take someone's pencil unless they say you can have it.

Let's imagine what they were thinking! "Whoa! Where did that rule come from? He must be crazy! This tradition has been passed down for ages, and it's always been done this way, so who is this guy to come along and make a new rule and tell me that I've been doing it wrong all my life." Oh, the anger and envy which arose in them! This is exactly what the Pharisees were going through and they were mad! They were mad these disciples were not doing what had always been done, and that Jesus wasn't making them follow the rules. If we want to take the envy slant here, the Pharisees possibly were envious the disciples didn't have to wash their hands, but they were still required to. Let's change the word to jealous now!

Somehow, I doubt Jesus was ever jealous of anything or anyone here on Earth. He had lived in Heaven with God all His life, forever.

He had helped God create everything. I'm certain there was nothing here that He wanted! So why was He even here? What in this world would ever possess Him to take on flesh and come to earth? Love! His true unjealous love for us was the only thing driving Him to do and be all He did and was. He loved those Pharisees just as much as He did the disciples, and His one desire was for them to believe in Him, who He was, and what He had come to do. He wanted them to understand it doesn't matter how much dirt we put into our bodies; it's our hearts that we need to keep clean. The way we do that is to live by God's laws, and not our own.

Our house was a one bedroom 12'x 40' trailer home. Eventually our parents built on a 16'x 24' living room which gave us a little more space, but I'm not sure you ever have enough space with five kids in the house. We slept in the living room, my two sisters and I on the hide-a-way couch, and my older brother on the other. I often ended up sleeping on the floor because being squished between your two older sisters, night after night, does not make for good sleeping habits. When my younger brother came along he slept with our parents.

The one bedroom had a closet with two drawers underneath, and a built-in dresser beside. My dad took out the dresser and put shelves in its place. I will never forget how happy I was to have my own private shelf to put all my clothes on. We didn't have many clothes, so it was more than plenty of room. There was also room for my shoes; I had one pair for school, and one pair for church. We usually only got one new pair of shoes each year at the beginning of school. We grew out of them by the following summer so we went barefoot until school started again. I had four sets of clothes and two dresses. The dresses hung in the closet and on the shelf, I would carefully fold and place together a different outfit for each day of the week.

One day my dad built us girls a three-way bunk-bed and placed it in the corner of the dining room. It was built of rough cedar and had slats that our foam mattresses lay on. When we felt like being alone, we could hang blankets or sheets around the outside by tucking them under the slats of the bed above. How good it felt to have our own space! I could carefully place each of my dolls and stuffed animals along the side against the wall and still have plenty of space to sleep. At first, I could set upright and had a perfect place to play. A couple of years later though, as I grew, my head began to bump the slats of the bunk above.

My bed started out on the bottom, my oldest sister, Elaine, slept in the middle, and Kate slept on top, but we all shuffled around a few times before we settled back in the spots we had started out with. Even though the beds were only twin sized, Kate and Elaine slept together a lot. Although there were often sister squabbles, they always seemed to me very close in their relationship and I was jealous of it, but at the same time I understood it because they were closer in age, and I was youngest.

Christmas and birthdays were a happy time for us because it was usually when we received the things we had been needing for a while; underwear, socks, snow boots, pajamas. Toys were not usually on the list of presents, but our parents would try their best to get us one. Our house was so small we didn't have room for a toy box, so whatever toys we did have, had to either remain in or near our beds or outside.

This lack of toys made me love to go to my cousin Lindsey's house because she had all the toys I wanted. We spent a lot of time at their house, or they at ours. Lindsey and I were only two weeks apart in age, she older than I. It seemed we were together all the time. We were second cousins, almost first cousins. My grandmother was her grandmother's aunt, and they had married brothers. So, my dad and her mom were almost double cousins, which made Lindsey and I second cousins, almost first cousins. Because of that, we were together not only at one family reunion, but also at the other. I was even closer related to my cousin George, because not only did this same situation exist with my dad and his mom, but also our grandparents on his dad's side and my mother's side were double cousins so that made George and I third cousins on one side and second cousins on the other.

Lindsey and I were great friends for many years and the orneriness flowed out of us on several occasions. Almost every time we were together our parents could count on us wanting to have a sleepover. As long as we got to be together, we didn't care whose house we were at. Most of the time her mother would say her room had to be cleaned first. We would set to the dreadful task; clothes and toys began to fly into their spots as quickly as they could. More than once we would just shove everything under the bed and pull the blanket down right to the floor to hide our dirty deed, and then pray her mother didn't look behind it, or that her little sister didn't tattle on us.

Family reunions were regularly at the park right down the road from my house. There was a creek we all played in that was well stocked with crawdads. It was usually a challenge to see who could catch the most or the biggest. On one particular day we went back to Lindsey's with some whoppers. I don't remember how many there were, but they were big enough we didn't need a lot. Lindsey's older sister had been especially grumpy with us that day and we were really angry at her, so when she began her bath water and went back into her room to get her clothes, we snuck into the bathroom and gave those crawdads a new home. The scream that came when she went back into the bathroom still rings in my head today.

Both of Lindsey's parents worked so they had the money to not only get them what they needed for Christmas and birthdays, but they also got what they wanted. The newest toys, the latest games, the nicest clothes, Lindsey had them all. I was so envious! It wasn't fair she always got everything and I had nothing. Often, I was ashamed to tell her or my other friends what gifts I had received because they all had already had the same thing for quite some time. As we began to get older, our friendship began to fade. I don't think my envy was the only reason, but it was certainly a lot of it. She was the prettiest cheerleader, the most popular girl, and dated the cutest guy in school. Being friends with her, despite the family tie, became too much for me and I couldn't take the jealousy in my heart, so I let the friendship die.

True Love does not Boast

So Pilate asked Jesus, "Are you the king of the Jews?" "You have said so," Jesus replied. Then Pilate announced to the chief priests and to the crowd, "I find no basis for a charge against this man." But they insisted, "He stirs up the people all over Judea by His teaching. He started in Galilee and has come all the way here." On hearing this, Pilate asked if the man was a Galilean. When he learned that Jesus was under Herod's jurisdiction, he sent Him to Herod, who was also in Jerusalem at that time. When Herod saw Jesus, he was greatly pleased because for a long time he had been wanting to see Him. From what he had heard about Him, he hoped to see Him perform a sign of some sort. He plied Him with many questions, but Jesus gave no answer.

Luke 23:3-9

Don't you just wish so bad you could have been there? I am certain that if I were, I would have got in their faces and told them all the things I had seen Jesus do; all the people healed or brought back to life, the sermon on the mount and the feeding of the five thousand. Then I would have tried my best to make Jesus do some kind of something amazing to prove to them He was truly the Son of God, the Messiah, just as He proclaimed. I know I could have kept Him from having to suffer those next horrific hours. Don't we all feel this way? And what would Jesus have said to us if we had attempted to protect Him that day? He would have said just what He said to Peter when he rebuked Jesus for telling the disciples He was going to suffer and die, "Get behind me Satan, you do not have in mind the concerns of God, but merely human concerns." Mark 8:33

If there had been a proper trial for Jesus, it would have probably taken some time. Jesus would have been in jail for a while. The disciples would have found all the people they could have to testify in His favor. Eventually Herod may have been forced to let Jesus go, and the cross might have never happened. But the events of that day had to happen, and Jesus knew it from the moment He became man. It was His destiny and His purpose! For Him to have given answer an Herod, to have told him all He had done, would have been defense, and He would have had plenty of it. He could have boasted of all the things He had done and performed something miraculous and probably walked away that day. But it was the concern of God, not man, Jesus had in mind.

In our small trailer home, there wasn't much room for anything unnecessary. We could play with our toys in the living room, if the weather was not suitable for outside play. One Christmas my older brother, Luke, had received a train set. He was so happy, and I was so jealous! It was huge and in my opinion the best gift any of us had ever gotten. But he was also very protective of it. I had begged him over and over to let me play with it, but he refused to even let me watch him while he did. Since it was so large, and there just wasn't room in the house, he had to set it up outside. The only place outside that worked was on top of the cellar.

Because of the trailer, my dad was terrified of storms. He had seen where tornadoes had totally taken away trailer homes, so any time there was a storm coming in he was glued to the television or standing outside watching the skies. I remember him often loading us all up in the truck in the middle of the night and taking us to Grandma's house. Only to load us back up an hour or two later to go home. Because of his fear of storms, he had a cellar built in the back yard. It was pretty big and the top was flat so it made a great place for the train to set.

One Spring Saturday when the weather was beginning to turn nice, our two cousins that lived just up the road came over to see Luke's gift. I couldn't believe he was going to let them come play with it when he wouldn't even let me be near it. I began to beg again and promised if he would just let me watch, I would not ask to touch it again. He reluctantly agreed and I was elated. I ran outside to help, so excited that I didn't even stop to put my shoes on. We had to stretch an extension cord from the barn to the cellar top to plug the train in. Luke told me to go inside the barn and hand the cord out to him through the window. I grabbed the old yellow cord, the one we always used for everything, plugged it in and began to stretch it across the dirt floor to the other side of the barn where the window was. As I pulled it, the cord got caught on the lid of the freezer. I began to swing it, trying to get it unhooked from the freezer lid. All of a sudden, that cord had a grip on me like nothing I had ever felt before. I had been shocked a couple of times at the ball field when us kids would go across the road and dare each other to touch the electric fence that held the bulls in, but I had never before felt this. I tried to let go of it, but it had a death grip on me and was not letting me even open my hand to release it. I began to scream Luke's name, as loudly and as fast as I could and time stopped as that cord shook me to the core of my inner being.

The next thing I saw was Luke coming in the barn door and unplugging it. Immediately I fell to the ground and lay there shaking and in a daze. What had just happened? I had no idea there was anything in the world that could hold onto a person that way. No matter how much I had tried to let go of the cord, my hand was stuck around it and there it stayed. Luke and my cousins came then and stood around me asking if I was ok. I just lay there crying in disbelief, realizing if Luke had not known what to do, or if he had not been so close, no one would have been there to rescue me.

They helped me to my feet and walked me to the house. My dad was in bed asleep because he was sick that day, and Luke woke him up to tell him what had happened. He looked at the blood on my hand where the cord had its death grip on me and his face turned ashen white. He knew the cord was old and it had some bare spots on it, but to tell us not to use it or to explain how dangerous it was, had not been something he had thought to do. He went out immediately and got the cord and fixed the bare spots. If he had had the money to throw it away and buy a new one, I am certain he would have.

I went to bed and stayed there for a few days. My mom talked about taking me to the doctor, but she knew at that point nothing could be done. I was just going to have to rest it off. I cried several times over those days, sometimes still feeling the after-effects of the electricity surging through my body and realizing how close to death I had been and was thankful for a brother who knew exactly what to do. As I told the story to my parents, I recalled screaming Luke's name over and over and how long it took him to come help me. He told me then the words were not coming out quickly, but slowly, and broken, and once he heard the sound of my voice, he knew exactly what was happening and what to do. The whole thing had only lasted a few seconds.

Over the next few weeks, I told the story several times to friends and family. I told them how Luke had saved my life, but I was confused why he never wanted to talk about it. I thought perhaps he felt bad he had asked me to stretch the cord instead of doing it himself. He could have boasted to everyone about how he had saved my life and how stupid I was to not have my shoes on and to be swinging it, and I should have seen the bare wires and known not to touch them. But he didn't! Just like Jesus, he acted out of love.

After that day, my brother became my protector, and I began

to have a respect for him I had not had before. Many times over the years he protected me from harm; from running all the way home when my knee was cut open, to pulling the girl off of me on the bus that was beating me up, he took care of me and never once do I remember him ever boasting about it. He did what was right at the time it was needed, and there's no boasting when you are acting in love.

True Love is not Proud

To some who were confident in their own righteousness and
looked down on everyone else, Jesus told this parable: "Two
men went up to the temple to pray, one a Pharisee and the
other a tax collector. The Pharisee stood by himself and prayed:
'God I thank you that I am not like other people—robbers,
evildoers, adulterers—or even like this tax collector. I fast
twice a week and give a tenth of all I get.' But the tax collector
stood at a distance. He would not even look up at heaven, but
beat his breast and said, 'God, have mercy on me, a sinner.'
I tell you that this man, rather than the other, went home
justified before God. For all those who exalt themselves, will be
humbled, and those who humble themselves will be exalted."
Luke 18:9-14

Ouch! This hurts me just reading it. How many times have I
thought in my heart I am so glad I am not like someone else.
Maybe they're disabled, or grew up poorer than I. Maybe they have
a skewed way of thinking, or their morals and values are different
than mine and I'm so glad my parents raised me better than that.
How many times I have thanked God I was not born in the starving
regions of Africa that we used to see daily on television.

The Bible doesn't tell us much about Jesus's family and upbringing. It doesn't let us know if His parents were poor or had money. It

does tell us His earthly father, Joseph, was a carpenter. If carpentry were then like it is now, it's a feast or famine existence. My husband and I have owned a carpentry business for twenty years, and it has either been rice or steak most of the time. But I like to think Jesus was well taken care of, and He had all He needed as a child. His dad was probably good at making He and His siblings wooden toys and nice furniture, and they may have each had their own bed. They probably lived in a decent house and ate well. I am confident God took good care of Joseph and Mary and their family and that Jesus didn't ever want for much.

But this parable gives us a look at two entirely different people living different lives. First is the Pharisee, dressed in all his finery. Standing tall and proud, shoulders back and chin held high, thanking God he is so different than other people. Proud that he has had a good upbringing, proud he has made better choices in life and hasn't had to suffer the consequences of bad decisions. He is proud he can walk to the temple and show God all his pride by praying out loud for how great he is.

Second is the tax collector. So humbled by his life he won't even get close to the temple because of his sin. So humbled God even allowed him to be able to walk to the temple to pray. So humbled that he wouldn't even turn to heaven to talk to God because he didn't want God looking at his face. Who knows what led him to become a tax collector? Just as today, no one likes the tax collector. We all cringe when that bill, higher and higher each year, comes in the mail and we want to call him up and ask how much more can he take from us. What circumstances were in this tax collector's life that made him continue in this job, knowing everyone hated him for his position?

But Jesus tells us the tax collector, in all his sin, was more righteous before God than the Pharisee in all his fancy clothing. What makes the tax collector more righteous? Clearly the Pharisee had a better position, he probably had more friends and everyone thought he was a great guy. So why was he not more justified to pray what he did? In Matthew 23:28 Jesus tells them, "In the same way, on the outside you appear to people as righteous but on the inside, you are full of hypocrisy and wickedness." Jesus looks right inside us and knows what's in there. He knows our thoughts and what our hearts long for.

This Pharisee needed to do some heart cleaning. He needed to put himself in the position of the tax collector and see things from his point of view. He needed to be forced to do that job for a while and see just what it was like. I always get so frustrated at people who judge others whose shoes they have never walked in. Maybe someone had an affair, we have no idea what the circumstances were that led them to that point. Maybe someone committed murder, until we have walked in that person's place, we have no clue why they took the life of another. Maybe someone stole a car or broke into a house, until we have lived the way that person has lived, we cannot make sound judgement as to what would drive that choice.

Jesus tells us in this parable if we are walking around with our nose to the sky, thinking that because we have not done the horrible things others have done, then our hearts are more wicked than those who actually have done these horrible acts but have come to God repentant, asking for mercy and forgiveness. Sometimes we forget self-righteousness and pride are sin, too. We like to think we have it all together, and there's no way we would or could ever live like others. Someone once told me, when I was being judgmental, to watch out, because if I ever thought something couldn't happen to me or that I was above it, then it would. And sure enough, it wasn't long later when I found myself in the exact position of the person I had been condemning. I was so blinded by my pride, just like this Pharisee, that I couldn't see the dirtiness of my own heart.

My siblings and I, the oldest four, were pretty close in age. Elaine, the oldest, was thirteen, Kate was twelve, Luke was ten, and I was eight when our little brother Thomas came along. I had been the youngest for eight years and if you have never been the youngest, you just cannot identify with how difficult that position is. Elaine and Kate had each other all the time. Luke always had friends or cousins to play with, and I was usually alone, just me and my dolls. Most of the time I was pretty happy with this situation. They were older and just didn't understand my type of play. Clearly, they had never been a little girl and had no idea how to play properly. Sometimes though, I wanted to join in on whatever game they were playing, but I was usually rejected. This would cause me to throw such a temper fit that our mom would make them let me play, which then usually turned into my losing interest or not paying close enough attention, and I was put out of the game very quickly.

On one such occasion Mom and Dad had went to the doctor's office for a monthly checkup. The drive was over an hour and so we had been at home most of the day alone when my brother and sisters decided to play Monopoly. Of course, I didn't want to be left out, but they kept refusing to let me play, so I went into my usual crying, screaming fit. But this time Mom wasn't home to referee. I stormed off to the bedroom, stomping and shouting all the way. As I went, I informed them that I couldn't wait to not be the youngest anymore so that they would have someone else to leave out instead of me. As I lay on the bed, having my fit, I thought to myself that I was finally not going to be the youngest anymore, and when I wanted to leave someone out, now I would be able to.

Thomas came the day before Christmas. My mother had decided that year she was not going to have us all shaking our gifts for weeks ahead of time, like we had always done in the past, so none of the gifts had names on them. When Christmas morning came, you can guess what happened. My mother was in the hospital and my father had no clue what was what or whose gift was whose. We ended up just all opening random gifts. Me being the littlest I don't have to tell you what I received, only two gifts were all I got to open, and neither one of them were mine. I couldn't understand why my mother had made such a huge mistake. When she got home, tempers were flying when she had to redistribute the gifts and I felt much better about the whole thing.

But the best gift we got that Christmas was a little brother. We went to the hospital later that day to see him, and I just stared through the window for as long as I could. I was in wonder at how amazing he was! Back in those days, kids were not allowed to hold the babies or to even be in the same room with them. The baby had to stay locked in the nursery behind that horrible glass window, and I wondered how much trouble I would get into if I just snuck in there to get a better look and touch his hand.

When he finally got to come home I was in awe! I had imagined over and over those nine months how great it would be to have a little brother to play with, but I had never once thought about him being so small. I had been envisioning a kid of four or five years old I could boss around and make behave or leave out when I wanted to, the way the others had done to me. It wasn't long before I began to feel terrible about the way I had felt about him. The mother in me came out quickly and I wished to be his mom so bad. He was so tiny and precious, and I was going to protect him with all I had within me.

As he grew up, I can honestly say Tom was one of my best friends. We did a lot of things together, and I can't think of anything I regret other than not spending more time with him during his teen years. The pride I felt before he was born at being able to be his big sister and bully him the way I had wanted to, quickly turned to love and protection. We were very close for a time and I am still very proud to be his big sister.

I realize these two types of pride; the pride of the Pharisee at how wonderful he thought he was, and my pride at not being the youngest anymore and having someone else be picked on, are two completely different types of pride. However, pride is pride and it can show its ugly face in many different forms. Whether at how great you think you are and feeling like everyone should follow your lead, or just being prideful that there will be someone else in the house to take on the role of being youngest, pride is still pride and it does not show love in any way.

True Love is Not Rude

When Jesus had finished these parables, He moved on from there.
Coming to His hometown, He began teaching the people in their
synagogue, and they were amazed. "Where did this man get this
wisdom and these miraculous powers?" they asked. "Isn't this the
carpenter's son? Isn't His mother's name Mary, and aren't His
brothers James, Joseph, Simon and Judas: Aren't all His sisters
with us? Where then did this man get all these things?" And they
took offense at Him. But Jesus said to them, "A prophet is not
without honor except in his own town and in his own home." And
He did not do many miracles there because of their lack of faith.
Matthew 13:53-58

I am going to assume most of you reading this book are Christians,
and that you have trusted Jesus as your Savior, and believe He
was the perfect sinless One. If you have faith and believe He never
sinned, then that means you must believe even as a child, He never
sinned. Take a look back at your own childhood and be honest and
recall all the times you found your sisters dime on the floor and
didn't tell her, or you used that extra dollar to buy a candy bar and
didn't tell your parents when they told you to bring back the change.

These people refused to believe Jesus could be the Savior who
had long been foretold was coming. They were His best friends, they
were the merchants that had seen Him be honest in all His dealings,

they were His friend's parents who had witnessed Him never telling a lie or being a bully or getting involved with the troublemakers in town. Yet when He had been gone for a while and had come back to town to tell them who He was and why He was here, they refused to look back at all He had done and believe Him. Their lack of faith kept them from witnessing and receiving many blessings.

We all know someone in our life that was just a rotten brat as a kid, yet when he or she grew up and left town for a while, they came back a different person; often a pastor or a minister. We wanted to think they have changed and become someone different, but in the back of our minds we still remember the ornery things they did, and we refuse to have faith they could be someone new. These people didn't have those memories. Jesus had never sinned so the fact they wouldn't believe in Him is even more distressing. It's downright rude!

As human beings, it is our nature to immediately think the worst about people. We have to train ourselves to think good of others. When someone new first comes to town, don't we keep them at a distance until we find out who they really are, and then we decide if we are going to let them into our circle? It's especially sad when this happens in our churches! Instead of immediately thinking they are there because they love God and want to be a part of a church that loves God too, we look at them in suspicion, and wonder who they are and why they have come. I know I am as guilty as anyone else at this. I must make myself walk up and say hello and tell them I am glad they are here. It's a difficult thing to do because many of us were taught as children to stay away from strangers, and then as adults we are told to not prejudge.

I like to look at these people that refused to listen to Jesus's teaching and say to them, "Y'all are so rude!" Then they could look right back at me and say the same thing. Our lack of faith, no matter how many years we have been a Christian, no matter how friendly we think we are, no matter how many times we have told our children not to be rude, makes us rude. If we want to show true love by not being rude, we must train ourselves to get over our suspicions and believe the best of people right off. Many times when someone is something other than what they say, the truth will come out later. But showing love is not rejecting them until they prove themselves, it's accepting them in faith and leaving the judgment to God.

My longing for love had begun as early in my life as I can recall. I had always wanted to be loved and that desire has driven many of my choices and decisions as I think it does for many people. Some of those decisions I wish I could take back, but some of them are actions that could happen to anyone and there should be no regret and no sadness when they come to mind. One such event happened when I was about ten.

Mother's Day was coming and our Sunday school teacher had given us an assignment to help us try to become closer to our mother's. She told us that for the week leading up to Mother's Day we were to write our mother a note every day telling her how much we loved her and appreciated her. I jumped on that idea wholeheartedly because I so longed for her attention. At this point my little brother had arrived, and he took most of her time. Since I was the youngest of the older four kids, and they had their own lives going on, much of my time was spent alone.

I did exactly as the teacher had told us to do and I left a note in different places each day. Under her pillow, on her bed cover, in the kitchen, wherever I could leave them I knew she would find them. She never acknowledged those notes, but I knew she got them and hoped she was happy about it. Mother's Day came and I was proud to be able to tell the teacher I had done what she told us to. So for the next week she gave us another job; we were to hug our mother and tell her we loved her every day.

I was super excited! I had been able to accomplish the first part of the assignment and now I was going to do this one too. I had a good excuse; the teacher had told us to do it! I made good grades in school and did all my work so I could do this too. I couldn't wait to get home that day and begin this new homework. I changed my clothes and sat on my bed for a few minutes trying to get up the nerve to do it. Affection was not a big thing in our house and this was kind of scary to me, but when I finally was able to muster the courage, my timing was off.

She was busy in the kitchen getting lunch ready. I waited till I thought I had an opening and I ran up to her and grabbed her around the middle and hugged for all I was worth. "I love you," I said. Immediately she pushed me away and replied, "What is all this nonsense about?" I backed away quickly and couldn't even mutter the words to explain what I had been up to. Nonsense? All week instead of being appreciative and loving my notes, it had all been nonsense to her. How my heart ached! It was many years before I told her I loved her again. I just couldn't get the courage to take the chance of my affection for her being taken as nonsense again.

Now as an adult I can look back and see the hurt she went through as a child herself, and I understand that showing love and affection was not something she had been brought up to do. She had lived a very difficult childhood and I will go into more detail about that in a later chapter. I know now, just as I hoped then, she did and does love me in the best way she knows how. She showed her love and care in other ways, just not in the way I longed for as a child.

As my own kids have grown and some of them have children of their own now, I know there are things I have said and done that have hurt their feelings and I wish I could take back. But this experience taught me that no matter how small or often they showed me their affection, I was never to make them feel like it was nonsense. We must always be on guard of our children's feelings, never being rude, but showing them kindness just as Jesus did throughout His life. We never get a second chance to control our words once they leave our mouths. We can apologize, but the initial hurt will always remain with that child.

True Love is Not Self-Seeking

Then Jesus was led by the Spirit into the wilderness to be tempted
by the devil. After fasting forty days and forty nights, He was
hungry. The tempter came to Him and said, "If you are the Son
of God, tell these stones to become bread." Jesus answered and
said, "It is written, 'Man shall not live on bread alone, but on
every Word that comes from the mouth of God.'" Then the devil
took Him to the holy city and had Him stand on the highest
point of the temple. "If you are the Son of God," he said, "throw
yourself down. For it is written, "' He will command His angels
concerning you, and they will lift you up in their hands, so that
you will not strike your foot against a stone.'" Jesus answered
him, "It is also written: 'Do not put the Lord your God to the
test.'" Again, the devil took Him to a very high mountain and
showed Him all the kingdoms of the world and their splendor.
"All this I will give you," he said, "if you will bow down and
worship me." Jesus said to him, "Away from me Satan, for it is
written: 'Worship the Lord your God and serve Him only.'"
Then the devil left Him and angels came and attended Him.
Matthew 4:1-11

Temptation presents itself to us all in different ways. What is
the driving force of temptation? In this situation for Jesus it
was the devil himself. That liar of liars! That cunning serpent who

"prowls around like a lion looking for someone to devour." 1 Peter 5:8. Could Satan have really given Jesus the world and its kingdoms if Jesus would have worshiped him? I doubt it, because it isn't his to give and Jesus knew that. Jesus's chief goal here on earth was to be perfect, to not sin at all, for us! We are the apple of His eye, the jewels of His heart and He knew He had to do this thing for us.

However, this was apparently not the only time Jesus was tempted. Hebrews 4:15 tells us, "For we do not have a high priest who is unable to empathize with our weaknesses, but we have one who has been tempted in every way, just as we are, yet He did not sin." This says to me that in Jesus's daily life, temptation was there. His mother didn't lock Him in a room and feed Him through a little hole to keep Him from ever having the chance to sin. He was out in the world, experiencing all that we experience, yet chose to keep His eye on the prize.

But Satan isn't the only driving force behind our sin. Sometimes, maybe most of the time, it's our own self-seeking that causes not only the sin, but also the temptation. James 1:14 & 15 tell us, "But each person is tempted when they are dragged away by their own evil desire and enticed. Then, after desire has conceived, it gives birth to sin; and sin, when it is full grown, gives birth to death." Do we really need these verses to tell us what we already know to be true? What a foolish people we are when we blame everyone else, including Satan, for our sin.

We are a selfish generation! But who can blame us? We have come upon a time when improving our way of living is our main focus. We build bigger and better houses so we can fit more stuff into them that we never use. We buy faster cars that have all the bells and whistles we can't live without. The health food and vitamin supplement industries are booming because we want to live longer and healthier. And when all these things still leave us lacking and longing for something bigger and better, we go looking for more. But what should we be looking for really?

James 4:7-8a say, "Submit yourselves, then, to God. Resist the devil, and he will flee from you. Come near to God and He will come near to you." If you have been in church at all in your life you should have been told that we need to have a daily time set aside to be with God. This is something that I have struggled to keep up my whole life. I can honestly say that I have never done a daily quiet time for an extended period of time, ever. I have good intentions, and I can start one and stay with it for a while, but then I get too busy and my quiet time is always the first thing to go in my schedule. But the Holy Spirit whispers to me every day that if I will come near to God, if I will spend a daily time of prayer and reading His Word, then I will find what I have been seeking all my life. He will fill the needs and desires that I struggle to break away from. He will take away my selfishness by helping me focus on His true, selfless love, not my own self-seeking ways.

We were poor and we knew it but as a child being poor isn't so bad as long as you have clothes and a bed and food. I was happy in our little trailer house, in my little bed or behind the couch. Many naps were taken behind that couch with my doll and her blanket that my grandmother had made. There was also a tree in the back yard that I spent a lot of time in. It was easy to climb and I would get as high as I could with my little blue song book full of hymns and sing for as long as the day would allow. We didn't have any video games and weren't allowed to watch much television so outside was our playground. As long as we had some sticks and mud or woods to explore and trees to climb, we were content.

But my desire to be loved loomed over me every day. My mother was always so busy, cooking and cleaning and washing. Rarely did she have time for me, and my dad was always away working. Sometimes his jobs were close and sometimes they were far away but no matter what time of day it was, I loved hearing his big, old, log truck coming down the road. He was always dirty and sweaty and even now I can still remember that oak smell, mixed with gas and oil, that clung to him every day.

He was a hard worker and taught us kids to work hard too. In the back corner of the house, where the trailer and the living room came together was the outside water faucet. Because of rocks and an electric line, we were not able to mow in that area. One day my dad told Luke, Kate and I to pull all those weeds. We didn't own a weed eater and the weeds had grown too big for the scissors that we normally used. As we stood there looking at those weeds, most of which were standing taller than we were, we asked our dad, more than once, if we had to pull them all. I don't know how many times we asked him that same question, but apparently it was more times than he was ready to answer yes to. Next thing we knew he had a switch and it wasn't long after that, the job was done.

Kate was dad's favorite. Our parents always claimed that they loved us all the same, but it was obvious that she was the apple of his eye. She always got to go everywhere with him and she usually came home with a candy bar and a pop. Oh, how I longed to be her! She was the smartest in her class, all the boys liked her, she could outrun them all or beat every one of them up. She was athletic and pretty. No wonder he loved her the most!

Every night when we went to bed my dad would always stand beside our bunk bed with his hands under her blanket for a long time. Since our bed was in the dining room, if my mother came into the room, he would walk away from the bed, either toward the kitchen or down the hallway toward the bathroom. I always felt so special the few times that he would lean down to the bottom bunk and give me an extra kiss. It was my hope that someday he would love me as much as he loved her.

That day finally came on a Saturday. It was a special day in our community and the town we lived in was having a celebration. My dad was going to wait and go in later so my mother took the other four kids and went on. I stayed behind with him, how special I felt that he picked me to stay instead of Kate. A few minutes after they had left, he sat down on the couch. He told me to come sit by him and the next thing I knew he had pulled me onto his lap, facing him. He then threw the blanket over us, just as I had seen him do with Kate many times before. He began to hold me and rub my back, just as I had seen him hold and rub her too. How special I felt! Finally, he loved me! Finally, I was the apple of his eye.

As I sat there though, his hands began to rub my back lower and lower. I wondered if Kate felt as uncomfortable as I was feeling right then when he had done this to her. I had never been told anything about my body being my body, or that no one was to touch it but me, but in that moment I knew that I was not okay with what was happening. I was sure though, that he had no idea how I was feeling. He was my father and he would never do anything to make me feel bad. I didn't want to tell him how I was feeling because this was my time of being special to him. I had waited so long for this moment that I wasn't about to ruin it by telling him to stop.

I had been in church and I knew what needed to be done to get out of a bad situation, so I began to pray. "Lord, get me out of this. Make this stop. Do something to make him realize I am feeling really bad right now." Just at that moment, those words had barely escaped my mind when the phone rang. I jumped up off that couch with all the force within me and ran to the phone. "Hello," I said. Again, and again, "Hello." But no one was there! Even though there was no one on the other end, I knew who had made that phone call that day. I told my dad then that it was probably time for us to leave and I decided I would never allow myself to be in a position where he could make me feel uncomfortable again. It was my fault that I couldn't tell him how I was feeling, but I was still so happy inside that he finally loved me as much as he loved her.

It happened a couple more times in different situations. We had cherry trees planted beside our house, and in the cool of the evening after dinner sometimes we would go outside because it was cooler than inside the house. One day it was just he and I sitting there across from each other. He had on cut off shorts, as he often did in the summer time, and he was exposing himself to me. I thought he didn't know, but as I sat there and he glared at me, I felt that uncomfortableness settling in again and I got up and left him to set there alone, feeling sorry for him that he didn't know he was showing.

The last time was in the log truck. It was always a treat that we all begged for, getting to go to the saw mill to deliver a load of logs with him, because on the way home, if we could dig enough change out of or from under the seat, he would stop at the dairy freeze and buy us an ice cream cone. I always wondered how so much change got in the seat and thought that he put it there on purpose for us to find. That day we had finished our ice cream and was on the way home, and he told me to scoot over beside him. Then he laid my head in his lap and began rubbing my back and bottom. Since I had decided this was not going to happen again, I only lay there a short time, and then I sat up and scooted back over to the door. I hated to hurt his feelings that way, and rejecting his love was difficult, but the urge to draw a line was stronger than being loved at that moment.

I was too young then to know the selfishness that was lurking inside my dad's heart in those days. It would not be long though before I learned. What I thought was true love I soon found out was not what I was getting from him at all. Selfishness looms in all of our hearts in some form or another. Yet another reason that we must have a Savior, another reason we must be forgiven of sin. Just as Jesus fought against the Devil as he was being tempted in the desert, we must also fight off the temptation of selfishness when it presents itself.

True Love is not Easily Angered

When it was almost time for the Jewish Passover, Jesus went up to Jerusalem. In the temple courts He found people selling cattle, sheep, and doves, and others setting at tables exchanging money. So He made a whip out of chords, and drove all from the temple courts, both sheep and cattle; He scattered the coins of the money changers and overturned their tables. To those who sold doves He said, "Get these out of here. Stop turning my Father's house into a market!" His disciples remembered that it is written, "Zeal for your house will consume me."
John 2:13-17

"**B**ut didn't Jesus sin when He got angry in the temple?" I have been asked this question by my church kids many times over the years and my answer to them is always the same. No, because there is such a thing as righteous anger. Then I put it to them this way: "If you walked into your house one day and there was a guy in there beating up your mother, wouldn't you get angry? Wouldn't you try to stop that guy any way you could? Wouldn't you call the police or find a ball bat or something in your anger? And would that be sin for you to try to protect your mother in your anger?"

This is the same thing Jesus went through. The temple was

a holy place, and the people had turned it into a money-making business, and that was not what God had intended for it to be at all. His zeal for the temple burned within Him, and He made things right. In fact, if we look at all four of the gospels on this matter, it never even says Jesus was angry when He did this. Matthew 21:12 & 13 Jesus entered the temple courts and drove out all who were buying and selling there. He overturned the tables of the money changers and the benches of those selling doves. "It is written," He said to them, "'My house will be called a house of prayer,' but you are making it a den of robbers." Mark 11:15-17 On reaching Jerusalem, Jesus entered the temple courts and began driving out those who were buying and selling there. He overturned the tables of the money changers and the benches of those selling doves, and would not allow anyone to carry merchandise through the temple courts. And as He taught them He said, "Is it not written, 'My house will be called a house of prayer for all nations.'? But you have made it a den of robbers." Luke 19:45 & 46 When Jesus entered the temple courts, He began to drive out those who were selling. "It is written," He said to them, "'My house will be a house of prayer,' but you have made it a den of robbers."

Was Jesus angry when all this took place? It doesn't say it in the text but this would be a question for my dear sweet friend, Dr. John Easton. He was a Greek scholar-yes, he was! When he preached and taught, he would read directly from his Greek Bible and it would say almost the exact same words as my Bible. Every now and then he would stop and say some translations said this or that, but what it really meant was... He would tell you all about the Greek language and the different tenses, and how they were used and understood. He actually was a teacher of Greek in different colleges in other countries. I wish he were here now so I could elaborate on this a little more, but he went to be with Jesus last year and I have missed him dearly since.

So I have to look at more scriptures on this subject of righteous anger. We know from several different instances, God was angry at the Israelites for different things they had done. In Numbers 22:22 God was angry at Balaam for disobeying. In Psalm 106:40 God was angry because the people had been worshiping idols. In Deuteronomy 1:34 God was angry with the Israelites for not trusting Him to take care of them as they entered the promised land. God is holy and righteous and this shows us He gets angry just like we do and since He is righteous, then his anger is also righteous. I do not believe it is sin to have a righteous anger, or in other words, an anger that is for the right reason.

Anger is a natural emotion given to us at the time of birth. I will never forget the screams of anger that came from my fifth-born child at the moment she came into this world. It was different than the other four, whose cries were that of being scared at all the newness. But number five, whoa! She was angry and wanted back where she had come from. The fire that was in her face said it all! She was a very lazy baby and in fact was so comfortable in her surroundings that the doctor had to actually put his hand on my tummy and push her down and out. It isn't the emotion of anger that is wrong, it's what we do with our anger that causes us to sin.

If we go ahead and assume from this text of scripture in Matthew that Jesus was angry when He did all of this, what was the results of His anger? Did He hurt anyone? It doesn't say so! Did He go on and on about it for days and complain and make it a point to throw back in their faces? It doesn't say He did. Did He scream and shout and call them names? Well, He called them robbers, stating exactly what they were doing to the people. Jesus simply made them leave the temple and reminded them a marketplace was not what the temple was intended for, but it was supposed to be a house of prayer. A place where the people could come and get right with God again.

At that time, before Jesus's ultimate sacrifice on the cross, certain sacrifices for different sins were still required. You can read about most of those in the book of Leviticus. The people would travel, sometimes long distances, to reach the temple and make their sacrifices to pay for their sins. Instead of bringing their animals with them, merchants had set up booths, if you will, to allow the people to buy their animal sacrifices, instead of bringing them all that way. Also, sometimes their money had to be exchanged into different currencies, hence the money changers. Jesus called them all robbers, which leads me to believe they were charging way too much for their goods and the money changers were cheating them out of the proper amounts.

This is the only place in scripture where we can assume that Jesus might have been angry, an anger that is clearly a righteous anger for God's house, the temple, and the dishonesty going on there. When we keep in mind His purpose here, and He had lived sinless, by faith we must believe that anger was not something He had an issue with. When we go off at those we claim to love in anger, we are not showing true love to them. Anger is something that over time we must learn to control. We must learn to tame it so we only feel it when it is a righteous anger, something we should be angry over, and even then, we must control our reactions to it.

It was a lazy summer day and I had been playing inside on my bed because it was hot outside. We had gotten a little window air conditioner in the living room and on really hot days Mom would turn it on. Sometimes she would hang a blanket over the door between it and the trailer house part and we were only allowed in there for a little while each day. We were required to stay outside at least one hour, no matter the temperature in the afternoon. I usually found any excuse I could to come back inside but most of the time was met with the command that my time was not up yet.

But this day I was laying on my bed when Kate and Dad came home. They had been to pick blackberries and Kate had gotten sick. Her face was red and swollen from crying, and she walked into the house and straight to the bathroom. Elaine saw her face too and quickly jumped up and followed her. Dad went to mom and kissed her and told her Kate had gotten sick. Mom tried over and over to get Kate to open the door and let her in, but she wouldn't. The bathroom was the only door in the house that had a lock on it, and was our only place to really be alone. Kate and Elaine stayed in there the whole rest of the day, and when it was finally bedtime, they came out and crawled into bed. After that Kate began to sleep with Elaine almost every night unless she was staying with a friend, which happened more and more often.

Kate was a Sophomore and Elaine was a Junior when school started that next year. We were busy all the time because they both played basketball and volleyball. I was in seventh grade and I also played basketball, and Luke did too. It was really important to my dad that we all were athletic and involved in sports. Before bed at night, he made us do exercises in the living room. The television would go off, and we each had to do sit ups and toe lifts and jumping jacks. It was often a competition to see who could do the most.

I worked hard to be as good at things as the other kids were. I so badly wanted my dad's attention and now that Kate and Elaine were staying gone more, I was getting it. I made sure that I didn't let myself get alone with him though, because the uncomfortableness of it was getting worse each time. But I was the apple of his eye now, and he took me with him now instead of the other girls. Luke went with him more often also and I felt glad for him that Dad loved him now too. Elaine and Kate had been gone more and more and I remember my mother getting angry that they were always wanting to stay somewhere else so much. Our house was small and we didn't have much, so I understood why they didn't want to be there.

One day in January, Mom came to the school and picked up Luke and me. We kept asking her what was going on and she wouldn't tell us until we were in our green and white Blazer. She told us she and Dad were getting divorced. We couldn't believe it! I was in a class with 25 other kids and only one of them had parents that were divorced. I couldn't believe I was going to be the next one. Luke and I just kept asking Mom why. Over and over we begged her to tell us! She didn't go home, instead she took us for a drive to the State Park and I remember seeing the huge herd of deer standing in the park that cool winter evening. I don't think I had ever seen so many at a time, and they were majestic in the evening light, the cold breath streaming from their nostrils. They just stood still as we drove by and didn't run away.

I don't remember how long we drove or have any clue how many times my brother asked her to please tell us why. I was frozen in fear as to what was going to happen to us. What was going to happen to Dad? I had finally won his love, and now it was going to be destroyed for a reason I may never know why. I felt so bad for him, and in those minutes, I wanted to run to him and tell him I loved him so much. We were almost home when my mother was finally able to utter the words, "Your Dad has been doing things to your sisters." I knew. I knew! My brother insisted on knowing what things, and he just kept hammering at my mother to tell him what things, but I knew. I didn't need an explanation. I had been watching it for a long time and I had begun to be the recipient of his "things" too and I knew.

Sitting in the back of the car the pain of his betrayal set in then, and I began to cry a cry so deep and so hard, I felt I was going to die right there. All I kept thinking over and over was that he didn't really love me. It wasn't true he had shown me, but only a lie all along. When we got home, I walked into the house in a mass of numbness. I don't remember how long it was that I didn't speak, I couldn't speak. Elaine and Kate weren't home and I didn't know where they were, but Luke was angry and he had all the questions and I only listened to the answers. They were at my aunt's house and were going to stay there for a while.

By the time we went back to school, I don't know if it was the next day or the next week, everyone there already knew my parents were getting divorced, and I was so ashamed and embarrassed. Divorce was not common back then and in a small town like ours, you knew that you were instantly the subject of the newest gossip. My friends badgered me to tell them why. They had heard their own parents talking, but it was all hush hush and they wanted to know why as bad as I had. I finally told one of them and begged her not to tell, and she assured me she wouldn't, but we all know how seventh grade girls can be and by the next day the whole class knew.

A side of my mother at that time emerged I had never seen before and I was both proud of her and disappointed. She began to take control of things, but at the same time she was a mess. My dad had gone to stay in a motel that his sister owned in the neighboring town and I wanted to see him so bad, but at the same time I wanted to punch him in the face. It was about two weeks before my mom took us there, and I couldn't believe what I saw. He was in a room alone all filled with beer cans and smoke. Most of the cans were empty and so were the cigarette boxes. My dad had always smoked or chewed but this was beyond anything I had ever seen him do.

He was setting in a chair and his face was red and swollen. His hair was a mess and so were his clothes, and it was clear he had experienced some sort of mental break down. I wondered if he had eaten and I wanted to hug him. Instead, I didn't say a word, but just went and sat on the bed as far away from him as I could. He talked a little bit to my mom and I could tell he was trying to be strong for Luke and Tom. I felt so sorry for him, but at the same time just kept thinking he was getting what he deserved for what he had done.

A few days later my mother told us he was going to move to his brother's house in Oregon and was taking Luke with him. I was sad to see Luke go, I would miss him, but was glad Dad was leaving so Elaine and Kate could come home. Elaine came, but Kate stayed away a few more days. Then one day my mother went and got her. She told her that a DHS worker was coming and she had to tell the worker that everything was ok at our house, otherwise she might take all of us away.

A week later Mom came once again to get me out of school. She had done this several times already so I didn't think it odd until we got home. She told me Dad had returned, and we would all be moving in with my aunt for a while, until we found somewhere else to live. I packed the few things I had and as we left there I wondered if I would ever see our little trailer again. My mother was different though, something had happened that she didn't want to share. The back door had been torn off the hinges and a window was broken. I asked her what had happened and all she would say was Dad had gotten mad at her because she wouldn't open the door for him. There was much more to that story though!

My aunt Susan had a little rock house that sat out in her front yard. Her granny had lived in it until she had to go to the nursing home, and it had sat empty for quite some time. My mother was able to get a loan to fix it up so we could live in it. She replaced the carpet, and we painted the walls. It was much bigger than our little trailer and although we still had to sleep on our bunk bed, at least we had it in a room of our own. Mom's bedroom was big enough for her and Tom to both have a bed, and Luke stayed with Dad.

But soon after, Mom became a mess emotionally and it was very difficult to see her that way. The stress of having four kids, a new job, taking care of a house and dealing with all the lies and rumors of a small-town scandal was taking its toll on her. Her moods were up and down and we never knew how she was going to be feeling at any given time. When she came home after work, she was on the phone until bed time with people calling her wanting to know what was going on and what she was doing about it.

Mom had taken Kate to another aunt's house and made her stay there. The aunt was elderly and lived just right down the block from us, so we could go see Kate whenever we wanted. I didn't un-derstand why Mom was so mad at Kate and didn't want her living with us during that time until a few years later. When my dad had come back from Oregon, he wanted the house back and he wanted his family back. He had told my mother Kate was lying about what had been going on. My dad was a good man, he was the only person I knew that would pick up a hitch-hiker and take him as far as his gas would allow. He was the only person I knew that would give a widow a break on the firewood he cut for her, because that's all the money she had. So along with my dad saying Kate was lying, everyone else in the community could not believe he was capable of doing such things, and they were also putting pressure on her not to believe Kate.

So, Moms anger at Kate continued to burn and when the elderly aunt had a stroke and was in the hospital, Mom had to go get Kate and bring her back home, her anger only got worse. She had started taking valium to help her deal, but I am certain she may have been better off without it. Through all this though, she continued to go to church and take us and tried her best to care for us, but the anger inside her was eating her alive and emerging as she didn't know how to cope. I decided because of her anger, and because she and Dad were divorcing, and because we were going to be ok, there was no reason for me to tell Mom that Dad had also done "things" to me. I didn't want to be the recipient of her anger too, and so I kept my mouth closed. Elaine also was keeping silent about what she had seen and knew, and we left Kate to make the stand alone.

True Love Keeps No Record of Wrong

At dawn He appeared again in the temple courts, where all the
people gathered around Him, and He sat down to teach them.
The teachers of the law and the Pharisees brought in a woman
caught in adultery. They made her stand before the group and said
to Jesus, "Teacher, this woman was caught in the act of adultery.
In the law Moses commanded us to stone such women. Now what
do you say?" They were using this question as a trap, in order to
have a basis for accusing Him. But Jesus bent down and started
to write on the ground with His finger. When they kept on
questioning Him, He straightened up and said to them, "Let any
one of you who is without sin be the first to throw a stone at her."
Again, He stooped down and wrote on the ground. At this, those
who heard began to go away one at a time, the older ones first,
until only Jesus was left, with the woman still standing there. Jesus
straightened up and asked her, "Woman, where are they? Has no
one condemned you?" "No one, sir," she said. "Then neither do I
condemn you," Jesus declared. "Go now and leave your life of sin."

John 8:2-11

The commandment these teachers of the law and Pharisees were
referring to here is found in Leviticus 20:10. However, they

left out one important part of it. It says, "If a man commits adultery with another man's wife—with the wife of his neighbor—both the adulterer and the adulteress are to be put to death." Wait, where is the man in this picture? I love a scene in a movie I saw where the Pharisees are shown paying the guy money who had been with this woman. They let him leave and then dragged her off to Jesus. That may or may not have happened, but scripture does tell us this was a trap because they wanted to accuse Jesus.

What did they want to accuse Him of and why? They had been trying for some time to find a reason to have Him arrested because so many of the people had been following Him and believing His message, and His answer to the Pharisees question could have been used against Him. If He answered that she should be stoned, then it would have gone against His message of love and forgiveness. But if He answered she should not be stoned, then He would have been going against the law of Moses. For years the temple leaders had kept the people under their thumbs with the law, I'm sure there was money in this equation somewhere, and they didn't want their way of life changed. But Jesus knew their hearts and their intent, and so He paused for a moment before He gave them an answer.

Have you ever wondered what He wrote on the ground? Dr. Easton thought maybe it could have been their sins. I wonder if He just wrote the word "SIN." Or maybe He was simpler and just drew an arrow in each of their directions. Whatever it was, the Bible doesn't tell us, so it wasn't important. What I think is most important is that He paused before He answered. How many times are we asked a question and just blurt out something we regret later? When He did answer, He gave them something to think about they hadn't expected.

Jesus didn't come to abolish the law of Moses, He actually added to it in places. On this particular subject in Matthew 5:27 & 28 Jesus tells us, "You have heard it was said, 'You shall not commit adultery.' But I tell you that anyone who looks at a woman lustfully has already committed adultery with her in his heart." I wonder how many of those guys were adulterers in their hearts, possibly daily, like Jesus described here. Clearly some of them were; all of them had some sort of sin they had not made atonement for, and so each had to walk away. I wish I could have seen their faces a few moments later when they realized He had spoiled another one of their plots.

Jesus was the Son of God, the Savior of the world. He could have very easily listed this woman's sins and made her beg for forgiveness, but that didn't happen. Instead, He simply told her to turn away from her life of sin. Many times, I want to point my finger at the ones who have hurt me and tell them to beg for forgiveness, but if I am going to live like a Christian, Christlike, then I must also not be ready to throw stones at those people. I must just say to them that I have forgiven them and let them go. I know right, easier said than done, and something I fail at miserably. I have heard it preached that someone who hurts you must ask for forgiveness before we are required to forgive, but Jesus never taught that. In fact, when asked how many times we should forgive someone, Jesus said we should forgive them seventy times seven. Four hundred and ninety times. In other words, over and over and over again, keeping no record of wrongs.

My mother was the oldest of eight children. Her mother and father, Mary Ann and Adam, had five kids; Betty, Hannah, Susan, Jay, and Emily. Adam's job kept him gone most of the time and the family moved around the country a lot because of his job but mostly lived in Colorado. Later on, Adam left them and Mary Ann then married Michael. They had three more girls, Belinda and Becky, polar-opposite twins, and then Melissa was the youngest.

Mary Ann was a good mother and always made sure they were well dressed and their hair was fixed nice. My mother used to tell us that when she was little, her mother would braid their hair so tight, so it would be curly the next day for school, that she would have terrible headaches and she always swore she would never braid our hair, and she never did. But Mary Ann had to work and often that left my mother in charge of the others. Anyone who knows anything about siblings and the oldest taking care of the younger ones can tell you that this situation leads to some very hurt feelings later on in life.

Because of this, there were many hard feelings between my mother and the other kids growing up because she had to take on the role of mother to them, instead of sister. But they were family and they understood the difficult position that my mother had been put in by their mother, and we always spent a lot of time together when I was a kid. My mother also had a bad allergy to milk. She didn't know this until she was older, and it wasn't until then that she realized it had been the reason for many of her health problems and migraine headaches.

After my mother and dad married, there was a house fire in which Emily had been badly burned and eventually died. Mary Ann and Michael had divorced, and she married again a few years later. She had found out he had been doing something that she felt there was only one answer to, and when he came home one evening from work, she had been waiting for him with a gun. There was a question as to what actually happened that evening, whether there had been a struggle or if it was an accident, but Mary Ann was the one who took the bullet. My mother had also endured a bad miscarriage about a year later, so depression had been something she was battling.

So when all this happened with my dad, and we had to move, and she had to get a job and all the stress that went with what was going on, Mom began to take valium, a popular antidepressant back then with side effects not yet known. She also began to make Kate take them. One day, at the little rock house, Kate was standing at the kitchen sink taking several of the pills at once. Elaine walked in and asked her what she was doing, and when she realized what was going on, she went to Susan's house and told her she and Kate were going to run away.

Later that evening after dinner, Susan came over to our house and told my mother she was going to have to pull herself together and start taking better care of us. My mother went off! She began screaming at Susan, and I came out of the bedroom then, and all I saw was hands flying and hair pulling. I ran out of the house and across the yard to get my uncle John. By the time John and I returned, they were setting on the floor calmly talking. I had never seen anyone fight before, especially those two. I didn't have any clue about the way they had grown up because they had always gotten along so well in front of me. It was the scariest thing I had ever experienced! Kate went to bed later and slept for two or three days, and I don't think anyone ever knew what she had done.

My mother seemed better for a while after that, and we lived in the little rock house for about a year. I liked it there! It had two doors on the front, and I always thought it was an odd way to build a house, but I liked it. We could either walk directly into our bedroom, bypassing Mom and whatever mood she was in that evening, or we could walk into the living room. It was only a block from the gas station, so anytime I had a dollar or two, a pop and a candy bar were only a minute away. I had never lived in town before, and I was very content there.

That summer I went to church camp. It was there I met my best friend Rachel. She was fun and energetic and became a wonderful light in my life. Each day after basketball practice, I would walk straight to the phone booth and call her. From the phone booth, it was only a quarter, but from the house it was long distance. We would talk for about an hour, until her mother came home and made her get off the phone. I also made other friends there that year who I still love and cherish, and I am thankful for the lights God sent into my life during that difficult time.

That same summer I also babysat a few kids and earned enough money to buy myself a bicycle. I had never had one of my own before and I was chomping at the bit as soon as I had enough to get it. My mother had traded the Blazer in for a Mustang because of the gas mileage difference, so she didn't have a way to bring the bike home. She told me my dad was going to do it, and I became really nervous because this was the first time he and I had spent any time together since we had moved into town. I got one of my friends to go with us, so I wasn't alone with him. It was a good trip because the ice had been broken between us, and I felt better about my dad after that.

Luke came over occasionally, and Dad began having regular visits with Tom. He never came to the house though, and us girls didn't see him much. Sometimes he would drive by on the road. I would see him go by and a mixture of emotions of being scared and wanting to hug him at the same time would overwhelm me, so I would go around back and climb the tree. I would stay up there watching the world go by for as long as I could. Trees were my solace and I was so thankful God had made them.

I was content and happy my aunt had let us live there to help us out during that time of our lives. I was glad she and mom were so close, and that I could spend so much time with my cousins. Susan could have very easily kept a record of all the wrongs my mother had done to her as a child and not allowed us to stay there. She could have kicked us out after that first fight they had, and we would have had to live somewhere else, but she didn't. She has always been a blessing to our lives, and I wish even today my mother could see this.

True Love Does Not Delight in Evil

"They tie up heavy, cumbersome loads and put them
on other people's shoulders, but they themselves are
not willing to lift a finger to move them."
Matthew 23:4

When we take a look at Jesus time here on Earth and all He stood for we must look at the evil that He most despised and stood against. Nothing stands out more to me than His constant dislike for the religious leaders of the temple of that day and how they did things. They were proud and expected everyone to look to them as the example for life. Jesus goes on in the rest of that chapter telling them all their sin and all they are doing wrong. Yet in verse 37 He tells them, "How often I have longed to gather your children together, as a hen gathers her chicks under her wings, and you are not willing." Even in their sin Jesus longs for them to come to Him and hide in His goodness, allowing Him to protect them and take care of them. But they had no desire to let Him into their lives.

So how does evil enter our hearts anyway? Why is it easier to do evil than to do good? How did evil enter the world? Let's go back to Genesis, shall we? In Genesis 2, verses 8 and 9 we see that, "Now the Lord God had planted a garden in the east, in Eden; and there

He had put the man He had formed. The Lord made all kinds of trees grow out of the ground—trees that were pleasing to the eye and good for food. In the middle of the garden were the tree of life and the tree of knowledge of good and evil." Then in verses 16 and 17 it says, "And the Lord God commanded the man, 'You are free to eat from any tree in the garden, but you must not eat from the tree of the knowledge of good and evil, for when you eat from it, you will certainly die.'"

Genesis 3, verses 1 through 7 then tells us this sad truth, "Now the serpent was more crafty than any of the wild animals the Lord God had made. He said to the woman, "Did God really say, 'You must not eat from any tree in the garden'?' The woman said to the serpent, "We may eat fruit from the trees in the garden, but God did say, 'You must not eat fruit from the tree that is in the middle of the garden, and you must not touch it, or you will die.'" "You will not certainly die," the serpent said to the woman. "For God knows that when you eat from it your eyes will be opened, and you will be like God, knowing good and evil." When the woman saw that the fruit of the tree was good for food, and pleasing to the eye, and also desirable for gaining wisdom, she took some and ate it. She also gave some to her husband, who was with her, and he ate it. Then the eyes of both of them were opened and they realized they were naked; so they sewed fig leaves together and made coverings for themselves."

From here when God comes along and knows what they have done and questions them about it, of course the man blames the woman, and then the woman blames the serpent. And evil and sin begin to take their place in this world. But why did God plant that tree in the first place? Why didn't He just forget about that one, or place it somewhere they would never go? Why didn't He put a tall wall around it so they could never get to it? For the same reasons we don't lock our own children in the basement, and tell them they are never going anywhere or doing anything so they won't ever have the chance to do anything bad or get into trouble.

I had a young woman living with me for a while who had a terrible disease. She happened to also have a four-year-old son. When I spoke to the father about them, he told me she would lock herself and the son in the bedroom for hours and not come out. They had only been with me for a couple of weeks at that time and I had not seen this happen yet, so I didn't really believe him. Then about a month into it, I discovered what he was talking about. Her son had done something really bad, and my daughter had flown off the handle at him, calling me to demand I come home to punish him. When I got here, it was clear I didn't need to punish him for some reason, so I just sat him on my lap and lectured him about destroying other people's stuff, and as a guest in someone else's home, we must respect their things.

I then went back to work, but when I came home, four hours later, she had done it. She had gone to her bedroom with him and there they had stayed. I tried to talk to her, but as she had done before, she just sat quietly in the corner, unable to explain her feelings or why she wouldn't come out, or let him come out. Asking God to show me what was going on, it hit me. This was the only way she could keep him out of trouble. He was a wild child, he was literally uncontrollable for her at that time, and this was her only means of keeping him from doing what all little boys do. So I explained to her that in order for him to learn the rules of right and wrong, in order for him to discover what he could and couldn't do, he had to be out and about discovering and learning. Staying locked in that bedroom wasn't going to teach him anything.

I believe God planted the tree of knowledge of good and evil for this same reason. He doesn't want a people who are robots, only doing what He tells them or allows them to do and no more. He wants us to be a people who choose to love Him and obey Him because we want to, not because He makes us. Notice that He said, "When you eat of it, you will die." He said "when", not if. He knew Adam and Eve would eventually eat of it. He knew the serpent was in that garden and would get to them some time. I wonder what would have happened if Eve would have kicked the serpent in the head or threw a big old rock on him? Would it still be just Adam and Eve here and no one else? Would they still be living in the garden alone?

These are questions we will never know the answer to, but what we do know is that it happened. And it happened just the way God knew it would. Evil entered the world and then sin. God wants us to choose to obey Him and to accept that Jesus died on the cross for our sins, therefore making a way for us to be forgiven of that sin and be able to come to heaven to be with Him forever. True love does not delight in evil and all the consequences of it. When we love someone, our actions will reflect it and evil will not be something we purposely do to that person.

The little rock house was a happy place for me, but the longer we stayed there, the more difficult it was for my mother. Since my aunt owned it, she told my mother that my dad was not allowed on the property. He began to come to the house to pick up Tom and it was usually just a quick stop, but one day he and Mom stood out on the front lawn and talked for a long time. As is customary in a small town, it got back to my aunt and when she informed my mother again that he was not allowed to be there, things became tense. We were not allowed to go over to her house anymore to visit, and soon after my mother purchased a house across town and we moved again.

This house was even bigger than the rock house, it had three bedrooms and a large bathroom- well, larger than anything we had ever had before. The kitchen was big and it also had two living rooms, one was right at the front door and the other sat off to the side. It had been the garage but the previous owners had turned it into another living room and that's where we spent most of our time. It was sunken into the ground so there were stairs that went down into it. For the first time in my life I had my own room and Elaine had hers, but Kate was still living with the woman from church. It had a small room off the laundry room that Luke would sleep in when he came to visit. Eventually he moved back in with us so my mom took the small room and gave him her bedroom.

My dad then began coming over more and more often. He usually always stayed outside and never came in. When he did come inside, it was very tense and us girls would go to our rooms or the bathroom. Elaine then got married right out of high school and Kate joined the Army so she was gone the summer between her junior and senior year. My mother was working second shift so if Tom was with my dad, I spent many evenings at my friend's houses. I had my bike and would ride all over town as long as I wanted. I learned to ride it without any hands and practiced as often as I could.

My mother realized how much time Luke and I were spending alone and it was a heavy burden for her, so she had our uncle Jay, her brother, move in with us. But he didn't care where we went or when we came back, all we had to do was tell him when we might be home and he was good. He also worked second shift as a bouncer at a local bar on the weekends so we still spent a lot of time alone. When he was home he sat around watching tv or his girlfriend was there, so it was fine with him that we were gone.

My mother and dad began spending more and more time together and I could see what was happening between them, but because of what had already taken place, I was sure that the unthinkable would never become reality. Dad would take us to eat pizza every Friday night, and then he bought season passes to the local theme park, something he had never done before. Sometimes he would take just my mother, but other times he would take me and my friend Sue along too. Sue and I loved it because as soon as we hit the front gate, we were on our own for the whole day. There were no cell phones back then, so checking in was not something we had to worry about. We spent the whole day chasing boys and riding the same rides over and over again.

One Saturday, in the fall, Kate and some friends came and got me and took me shopping. It was weird to me she did this because she hated coming to the house. I had only been seeing her at school and for her to just come get me to spend the day was strange. We went shopping and while there we ran into someone we knew from our town. She said that she had seen in the paper where my mother and dad were getting married again and wanted to know when it was going to take place. Kate told her it was happening that day. I knew nothing about it.

Upon seeing the look on my face, they all knew the shock I was feeling. Never, ever, ever did I ever imagine that my mother would marry him again after what he had done. The hurt of betrayal, not only from him, but also from her at that moment immediately sent me into angry tears. The woman who had spoken out apologized, and I was furious at Kate that she or no one else had told me. When we got home, I didn't even go inside, but I got on my bike and rode. I wanted to ride to the ends of the earth. I wanted to get as far away from both of them as the road would take me. But I had no money, and I knew the evil that lurked in the world, so I just rode to another friends' house. When I got there her parents also knew what was happening and when they seemed happy, I quickly produced more tears and it was not spoken about the rest of the evening.

The anger set in for me then. How they could do this without considering my feelings, how could the rest of the world know and I didn't, and how she could love him again without regard to what he had done was more than I could take. I was furious at the evil that had taken place without my approval. I walked around in a daze, angry at the world. It reflected in my friendships and in my school work and with my teachers. I was mad and I wanted everyone to know it and to feel my anger too. It was confirmation to me that neither one of them loved me at all, and never would.

It was at this time I decided there had to be someone out there in the world who would love me. I still had my dream of finding my prince charming and so my search began. Any boy who even looked my way, I was sure was him. When a relationship was short lived, I was devastated but would move on quickly to someone else because I was sure my true love was there. I prayed over and over God would send him to me so I could get away from my parents as soon as possible. I was only a freshman in high school, but I didn't care if I ever finished, I just wanted to be away from where I was.

True Love Rejoices with the Truth

Upon His arrival, Jesus found that Lazarus had already been in the tomb for four days. Now Bethany was less than two miles from Jerusalem, and many Jews had come to Martha and Mary to comfort them in the loss of their brother. When Martha heard that Jesus was coming, she went out to meet Him, but Mary stayed at home. "Lord," Martha said to Jesus, "If you had been here, my brother would not have died. But I know that even now God will give you whatever you ask." Jesus said to her, "Your brother will rise again." Martha answered, "I know he will rise again in the resurrection at the last day." Jesus said to her, "I am the resurrection and the life. The one who believes in me will live, even though they die; and whoever lives by believing in me, will never die. Do you believe this?" "Yes, Lord," she replied, "I believe that you are the Messiah, the Son of God, who is to come into the world." After she had said this, she went back and called her sister Mary aside. "The teacher is here," she said, "and is asking for you."

John 11:17-28

Now why do you think Martha told Mary that Jesus was asking for her? It doesn't tell us in the text Jesus asked her to go get Mary and bring her to Him. So why did Martha tell Mary this? Was it a lie? I believe when Jesus told her that Lazarus would live again, and she understood he would live once the resurrection happened, but then realized He was telling her Lazarus was going to live again right then, she rejoiced at this truth. She was so at peace and happy, she wanted to share this with Mary and was saying to her that Jesus had something important to tell her. She may have known Mary was upset at Jesus for not showing up before Lazarus had died, and would not have went to Him unless she told her Jesus wanted her.

We know from scripture this was the same Mary that, when Jesus was at their house, sat at His feet instead of helping Martha in the kitchen. She had been so enthralled with Him she didn't care what her duties were. She didn't care that Martha was having to do everything on her own, all she wanted was to be at Jesus feet, listening to His words. Now, she was angry with Him, so angry that she wouldn't even go out with Martha to meet Him. The one man she knew could have saved her brother's life, and she was mad at Him. Now, she just wanted to stay in the house and mourn for Lazarus. But then Martha showed up and told her Jesus was asking for her.

When Mary got to Jesus, she let her anger show. "This is all your fault!" she shouted. Well, what it really says in verse 32 is, "Lord, if you had been here, my brother would not have died." Again, "It's all your fault!" Scripture doesn't say she was angry, but I can hear it in her accusation. I know I would have been angry if the one person who could have saved my brother didn't come back in time. Jesus had actually delayed His coming back for two more days. One reason He may have waited so long is because "the Jews believed that the spirit didn't leave the body until the person had been dead for three days." (Dexter, 2017) He tells us in verses 4 and 15 that He did this in order to prove to them who He was so they would believe in Him, therefore, He waited until all doubt was gone that Lazarus was dead.

It doesn't tell us then how Mary and Martha reacted when Lazarus was raised back to life but we can assume they were very happy. Back in those days, as a rule, it was customary for the man to take care of the women in the household. If this were true in this case, then Lazarus death for Mary and Martha would not have been good news. They would have had to find other means of support. His resurrection meant that life could continue on the way it had been. Mary and Martha knew however, Jesus could have prevented the death in the first place. So, when He finally showed up and raised Lazarus back to life, they had to accept and believe this whole thing happened so God could be glorified and the people would believe Jesus was sent by Him.

We see Mary's rejoicing in the truth in the next chapter. John 12:3-7 says, "Then Mary took about a pint of pure nard, and expensive perfume; she poured it on Jesus's feet and wiped His feet with her hair; and the house was filled with the fragrance of the perfume. But one of His disciples, Judas Iscariot, who was later to betray Him, objected, 'Why wasn't this perfume sold and the money given to the poor? It was worth a year's wages. He did not say this because he cared about the poor, but because he was a thief; as keeper of the money bag, he used to help himself to what was put into it. 'Leave her alone,' Jesus replied. 'It was intended that she should save this perfume for the day of my burial.'" There are many opinions as to why Mary did this before Jesus death, but I believe it was because she was so grateful for all Jesus was and His true love for them that she couldn't wait until His death to do this for Him. She wanted to return His love while He was still alive, while she still had the chance to show her true love for Him.

I always loved when school was out for the summer. Usually my mom's twin sisters, Belinda and Becky, and their youngest sister Melissa came in to stay with us and my aunt Susan for a month or two. It was such a fun time! Becky was crazy and regularly pulled ornery pranks on everyone. We loved her and all her crazy fun antics.

Belinda was laid back and sensible. She was always the rule keeper and the disciplinarian. But we loved them both the same even if they were such opposites. Melissa was kind and sweet and loving to all of us and most of the time would just laugh at Becky and Belinda's constant disagreements.

When they were here, Sunday's were spent with family or doing something fun. Dad worked most Saturday's, unless it was too hot, so after church on Sunday we would load up in his old blue Ford pick-up and set out for a day of family fun. Often, we would gather all our stuff and mom would pack our lunch and we'd head out for the lake. Back then it was ok to throw the kids in the back of the truck and drive thirty miles down the highway to the lake. I loved the wind in my hair and always picked the back if there was a choice, but it was a long hot drive and by the time we got there we were ready for the water.

My dad was adamant that we all learned how to swim so that we wouldn't drown. Once there, he would make us each grab onto his back as he swum us out to the buoys to teach us how to swim. This day I was little, maybe four or five, and after standing back, far enough that he couldn't reach me, I watched as he took each of the older three out and gave them their lesson and brought them back. I was not ready though to learn, and if he came in my direction at all I would run away screaming and crying. I was so scared of the water and had no desire to learn to swim.

After he gave up the chase and went to have some fun of his own, I slowly ventured into the water, keeping a safe distance. I found a little sandwich baggie and began playing with it. What fun I had filling it with water and dumping it out again. I had been playing with it for some time when it suddenly got away from me. As it floated out further and further, I was sure that if I reached out just a little further, I could get it. All of a sudden, I tripped over something and down into the water I went. It was deeper than my head, but I could feel the bottom just under me. As I tried to bounce myself back toward the shallow water, I felt with my foot a wall.

Each time I tried to put my foot on the wall, I only ended up pushing myself further and further out. I realized that I couldn't get back onto the wall, so I began to cry for help. No one was near me though, and they were all having fun of their own, and each time I screamed I only ended up swallowing more and more water. I could see my mother up on the shore talking to one of my aunts, and I kept trying to wave my hands at her. Each time I went under, I would push with my feet and could jump up just high enough to get another breath of air. The whole thing lasted probably less than a few minutes, but at the time it seemed like I would be bouncing there forever or I was going to die.

I decided if I was going to die, I was going to go out fighting. I thought about how sad they would all be when they realized I was dead, and they would regret my not being there. I could see my mother sitting there and a few times I thought she would look at me so I would try to wave, but then she would look away again. Then suddenly, she jumped up and came to get me. All I could wonder was what had taken her so long? By the time she got there I was convinced that she had wanted me to drown and was leaving me there on purpose. Once on shore, I began to throw up all the water I had swallowed, and it wasn't until then that they realized how long I had been out there.

Now, here I was again drowning in my anger and my mother didn't care. She was happy again, and I was certain that was all that mattered to her. My anger though, was eating me alive! When my parents were home, I went into my room and stayed there with the door locked. When it was supper time, I ate in my room. Mom was still working second shift, so as soon as my dad came home from work to be with Tom, I would leave on my bike and not come back until dark. I purposed in my heart he was not my dad, and was never going to tell me what to do again.

One morning my mother cornered me in the bathroom and tried to talk to me. All I could do was scream and cry because I couldn't believe she had married him again. She tried to convince me he had not done those "things" because he had not admitted it to her. She told me Kate had lied about it all, and that Dad was a good man and would never do something like that. But I knew different! I told her I had seen it with my own eyes, but she wouldn't listen to me and instead insisted Kate had put it all in my head and it wasn't true.

Later that week, as I stood in the kitchen after school holding her full bottle of valium, I remembered the lake, and how I wished so bad I had died then so I wouldn't have to go through all this hate and anger now. I didn't want to feel this way about my mother and father. I wanted our family to be ok and happy, but it wasn't, and I was angry. I thought about the time my grandfather's dog had attacked me when I got too close to his face, and wished that I had died then. As I stood there holding that bottle, crying, I knew I could end it right then; if only it weren't for my dad.

He had always believed if you were a Christian, God would not allow you to become so miserable that you would commit suicide. I had heard him argue his point so many times that it had stuck in my head, and if I were to do it right then, he would believe I had went to hell and I didn't want anyone to think that of me. I had been in church and prayed the prayer, lately I had prayed it over and over, along with asking God to take me then and get me out of what I was going through. I thought I was saved, at least I hoped I was, so if I were to swallow that whole bottle and what my dad believed was true, then I must not be saved. Dad was being very respectful of me and my privacy at that time, but I didn't care. I hated him and I wanted all this shame and misery to be over.

One day, when he came home, I had been waiting for him so I could leave. Riding my bike around town was my out, and I did it as often as I could. Sometimes I would ride right down the middle of the road and wish someone would come along and end it for me. Other times I would ride as fast as I could with no hands hoping I would hit a rock and topple off head first and the nightmare would be over. This day though, changed all that for me. As I went out the drive, he was standing there at the back of his truck. He reached out and grabbed my arm as I went by and stopped me. "Priscilla, can we please talk?" he asked. I didn't want to talk to him ever again. I knew what he had done, and now I knew he was lying to my mother and I hated everything that he was.

I stopped my bike and couldn't respond to his question, but just stood there looking at him with all the hate I could muster. "I want you to know that I would put a gun to my head and pull the trigger before I would ever hurt you girls again," he said. What??? Did he just admit to me what he had done? Did he really just tell me he would kill himself before he would touch us again? I looked into his eyes then and the tears and regret I saw there was all it took for my hate and anger to instantly melt. In that moment, I didn't care he hadn't told my mother, he had just admitted it to me. The heaviness in my heart was gone then, and again I couldn't respond to him, but just rode away with a new sense of joy that I hadn't ever felt before. I was truly rejoicing in his truth. All the anger was gone and I felt like I could live and love him again.

True Love Always Protects

Shadrach, Meshach, and Abednego replied to him, "King Nebuchadnezzar, we do not need to defend ourselves in this matter. If we are thrown into the blazing furnace, the God we serve is able to deliver us from it, and He will deliver us from Your Majesty's hand. And even if He does not, we want you to know, Your Majesty, that we will not serve your gods or worship the image of gold you have set up." Then King Nebuchadnezzar was furious with Shadrach, Meshach, and Abednego, and his attitude toward them changed. He ordered the furnace heated seven times hotter than usual and commanded some of the strongest soldiers in his army to tie up Shadrach, Meshach, and Abednego and throw them into the blazing furnace. So these men, wearing their robes, trousers, turbans and other clothes, were bound and thrown into the blazing furnace. The king's command was so urgent and the furnace so hot that the flames of the fire killed the soldiers who took up Shadrach, Meshach, and Abednego. And these three men, firmly tied, fell into the blazing furnace. Then King Nebuchadnezzar leaped to his feet in amazement and asked his advisers, "Weren't there three men that we tied up and threw into the fire?" They replied, "Certainly, Your Majesty." He said, "Look, I see four men walking around in the fire, unbound and unharmed, and the fourth looks like a son of the gods." Nebuchadnezzar then approached the opening of the blazing furnace and shouted, "Shadrach, Meshach, and

Abednego, servants of the Most High God, come out! Come
here!" So Shadrach, Meshach, and Abednego came out of
the fire and the satraps, prefects, governors and royal advisers
crowded around them. They saw that the fire had not harmed
their bodies; nor was a hair of their heads singed; their robes
were not scorched and there was no smell of fire on them.
Then Nebuchadnezzar said, "Praise be to the God of Shadrach,
Meshach, and Abednego, who has sent His angel and rescued His
servants! They trusted in Him and defied the king's command
and were willing to give up their lives rather than serve or
worship any god except their own God. Therefore, I decree
that the people of any nation or language who say anything
against the God of Shadrach, Meshach, and Abednego be cut
into pieces and their houses be turned into piles of rubble, for
no other god can save in this way." Then the king promoted
Shadrach, Meshach and Abednego in the province of Babylon.
Daniel 3:16-30

Who was the fourth man walking around in the furnace? I had
always heard that it was Jesus Christ and I know many still
teach that, and for it to be Him would not be out of His character
at all. But in researching this scripture, I have found that there are
many different opinions out there about whether this was truly the
Son of God, or if it was just an angel. Both statements were made
by King Nebuchadnezzar, who at the time, clearly was more into
himself than anything else, so His judgement on this matter was not
a Godly one. It wasn't until after this event he began to follow God
and may have had better insight.

So let's take a look at some other scriptures which show us that
Jesus, in love, protects us. In John 17 Jesus prays that God will
protect His disciples, the ones God gave to Him, since He would

be leaving them and would not be able to do it any longer. Verse 12 tells us He protected them and kept them safe by the name God gave Him. Matthew 8 tells us about Him calming the storm that had arisen when He and the disciples were out on the boat. In Matthew 14 we can read about Jesus feeding the five thousand people so they wouldn't go hungry. And all throughout the gospels we can see where He healed the sick and drove out demons.

John 1:18 tells us that, "No one has ever seen God, but the one and only Son, who is Himself God, and is in closest relationship with the Father, has made Him known." Looking back then at Shadrach, Meshach, and Abednego, we know God protected them from the fire. So to say this was Jesus, "Who is Himself God," standing in the flames with them, in my opinion, is not a stretch. And even if it was just an angel, God was still the protector that had sent this angel. I have said it over and over again that Jesus's one goal here on earth was to live a perfect, sinless life so He could be the ultimate sacrifice for our sin, and we could have a way to get to Heaven to be with Him for eternity. He did this because of His perfect true love for us, and His one goal was and is to protect us from the flames of hell which await those who chose not to believe.

We had a neighbor man that was also our distant cousin, twice removed on our father's side, and possibly our mother's too, or something like that and his name was Don. I loved going to Don's farm! He truly was an Old MacDonald. Most of the time he had every farm animal you could want to see. Ducks, geese, hens, sheep, goats, cows, dogs; I loved them all. He lived between us and our grandmother, so we always walked by his house. Lots of times when he saw us going by, he would wave us to come on down to the barn so we could see the newest baby that had just arrived.

He lived at the bottom of the hill just where the road forked. You could take the bottom holler road to get to town, or you could take the upper road which was the one we lived on. One day as we were riding our bikes to grandmas with the neighbor kids, Luke's pant leg got caught in the chain of his bike. He had to stop where he was in the middle of that fork in the road directly in front of Don's house. The biggest neighbor kid was much older than we were so he tried to help Luke get the pant leg out, but it was stuck in there too tight. Just at that moment we could hear a car coming. It was scary to be right there at the fork because it was also on a corner, and the cars coming from the lower road couldn't see around the corner until they were right in the fork.

This was where Luke was laying, and as the car approached closer and closer, we girls were screaming for him to get out of the road. Not only was the neighbor boy much older, but he was also much bigger. So he picked Luke up, bike and all, and drug them to the side of the road, just as the car came by. But it was Old Don, and he simply turned into his drive just as they were clearing the road, and then came up to help Luke get free. Any time we needed help, we knew Don could and would help us. He fixed our bike tires numerous times through the years, always dropping whatever chore he was doing at the moment to make time for us.

He lived on that farm with his mother and my parents would warn us not to get too close to her because she would pinch you. I was a young teen before this happened to me. I had talked to her many times and had grown quite comfortable with her. My dad and I were standing in the kitchen talking to Don one day when she walked in behind me and gave me a good one on the back of the arm. When I flinched, and turned to look at her, she just smiled and giggled. Two lessons learned; not only don't get too close, but also know where she is at all times.

It was after dark one icy winter evening when our other neighbor man, Don's nephew Jim, came knocking on our door. We opened it and he was terribly upset. Someone had called him saying that something was wrong with Don. As he was driving down there, way too fast, he met another car and his bronco skidded and flipped into a corner. Another neighbor brought Jim to our house, and my dad drove him on to Don's. Don had been going to feed the cows their hay with the tractor. When he stepped down off the tractor, he slipped on the ice and fell, grabbing the gear shift as he slid and the tractor rolled over him. It was a couple of hours later before someone found him.

One of Don's dogs, a border collie, was truly his best friend and went everywhere with him. When Don was found, the dog was right by his side and wouldn't let anyone near him. They had to call in someone else to get him away so the EMT's could do what needed to be done. At Don's funeral, I cried and cried because all I could think about was how Don had come around the corner that day and turned into his drive, then came up and helped with Luke's bike. Also, how Don's dog had protected him from the rescuers, and I was so grateful his dog had loved him so much.

Things were good now at our house. My parents had remarried and my mother was happy. I had forgiven my dad for what he had done and trusted him that he would never hurt us again, and he didn't. I didn't see any need to try to convince my mother that my dad was lying to her about it; to do so would only make her mad at me, and unhappy again.

It was Kate's senior year of high school and she was still living with the lady from church, but shortly after Mom and Dad remarried, she decided to move back in with us. Kate had her own room and was still gone much of the time. But on the nights she was home, she always insisted that I sleep with her. I didn't want to sleep with her! I had always slept alone and sleeping with someone else was difficult for me. When I would ask her why, she just said she had really bad nightmares and was scared, but the truth of it was that she was worried Dad would "hurt" me and she felt like she needed to be there to protect me from him.

I had also been having recurring nightmares. It was always the same and would keep me awake for hours at night. It was set in the corral which was behind the little trailer we had lived in, and I was standing in the center of it. There were demons all around me, and they were constantly chasing me and trying to grab me, and when I would try to climb over the fence, there were snakes on the top rails, and I was too scared to go past them. I thought I was a Christian, so why was I still dreaming this. I went to see my pastor about it and told him I was scared that I might not be saved. He asked me if I had prayed the prayer of salvation and when I told him I had, over and over, he said that sometimes the Devil makes you have doubts and that was probably where the dreams were coming from. He told me to pray when I had the dreams, but it didn't help.

So I was glad to be sleeping with Kate. I was helping her, and she was helping me. But as we laid there at night trying to get to sleep, she would talk to me. She began to tell me of some of the things Dad had done to her and I learned the awful truth about what had happened the day that she had come home sick from picking blackberries. She said the reason she had told on him was because he had been leaving her alone and she was afraid he was going to start doing it to me. She was insistent that Mom had known about it all along and she asked me if he had done anything to me. I told her no because he had not done to me what he had done to her. I was afraid if I told her yes, then she might be mad at me for not telling Mom, and letting her take all the blame. Also, she had undergone much scrutiny and rumors because so many people said she was lying, and I didn't want that stigma.

I was glad to have Kate home again, but she and mom still could not get along. Most days they just didn't talk at all so it wouldn't end up in a fight. Kate had been dating someone seriously for about a year and so in January of her senior year, she got married and moved out again. They lived in a neighboring town, but she continued to finish her school there where we had grown up. I was sad for her to go and shortly after she moved out, we moved back into our little trailer home in the country. Her protection of me made me feel loved, and just like Don's dog, I knew she would always be there for me.

True Love Always Trusts

Going a little farther, He fell to the ground and prayed
that if possible the hour might pass from Him. "Abba,
Father," He said, "everything is possible for you. Take this
cup from me. Yet, not what I will, but what you will."
Mark 14:35-36

O h, how many times over the years I have prayed and asked
God to take this cup from me. Have we not all been there at
some point in our lives? Why do we have to even face trials in our
lives anyway? Jesus was about to face His biggest trial, and He was
not looking forward to it. He knew all the prophesies about Him and
He knew what was about to begin in just a few hours' time. His heart
was hurting and He asked God the Father to please find another
way. He had prepared all His life for this moment and it was going
to be the most difficult thing He had faced yet. But I don't believe
it was the pain He was dreading, I believe that His fear was in the
fact He still had a few hours, His most difficult hours ever, that He
had to maintain sinlessness.

If it were me, and I knew what was about to happen, you can
bet I would have rented, or stolen, the fastest camel I could have
found and gotten out of Jerusalem as quickly as possible. I would
have been Jonah and ran. But not Jesus! He had endured so many
years of temptation and trial and had overcome each one without

sin, and now that the biggest trial of them all was staring Him in the face, if He sinned, even once, all His efforts would have been for nothing. I believe it was in these moments that "The Lord laid on Him the iniquity of us all," Isaiah 53:6. It was a huge burden to bear the weight of the sin of the world and it was here, just before it would all be finished, He was feeling it the most.

If you have ever trained for a long race, you know the most difficult part is the run in the middle. You trained for a long time and have prepared for months, but when you get to the middle part of the race, your body becomes tired and you want to just stop and walk for a little while. But if you push on through, and you keep up the pace and don't give up, eventually your body will adjust and you will get that second wind you know is coming, and you can finish the race strong. This time in the garden was that difficult middle time for Jesus, that time just before the end and the race would be finished.

As the next few hours unfolded, even though God did not make another way, Jesus maintained His goal. He knew if He could just get through it, silently and humbly, then it would be over and the way for us would be made. All we have to do now is to believe in what He came to earth for, to trust Him as our Savior, just as He trusted God to get Him through what was about to happen. He told God if there was no other way, then He would endure it to the end. His true love for us was in His trust in God to make all things right through His life.

We attended the local Baptist church and were there most of the time. We didn't go when there was an upset in the church, as often happens when people are trying to run things. We had some really good pastors and Sunday school teachers, and so I heard the Gospel of Jesus Christ regularly. I knew I needed to give my heart and life to Him, but I thought the only way to do it was to walk forward during the invitation with everyone watching. I was terrified to do that! I didn't want anyone looking at me and knowing what I was doing.

I decided when my cousin Mitch went forward, I would go at the same time. It just so happened that we were not there the Sunday he went. I had to change my plans and so I figured when Lindsey went, I would go with her. She also happened to take that walk when we weren't there. Some months later I finally found the courage to step out on my own. I went forward and with a deacon prayed the prayer of salvation. On the way home, I remember hoping I wasn't going to hell now, I didn't feel the security that comes from truly giving your heart to Jesus.

The reason I had went forward was out of my extreme fear of Hell and Satan. Many times, when I heard about being saved, along with that message came this fear of spending eternity in Hell. The images told to me had painted such a vivid picture in my mind; I never wanted to go there. But it's not a fear of Hell that should drive you to become a Christian. An extreme desire to follow Christ's example and live for Him should be the only reason for salvation. Any other motivation for becoming a Christian is wrong and won't bring you to God.

As time went on and I continued to attempt to grow in the Christian faith, all I found myself doing was struggling to make the right choices. I felt a continual drawing to Jesus, but I could never get close enough to feel like my salvation had actually been real. As a teen, we had a youth revival in our church, and an amazing youth evangelist came. Several of my friends came, and many of them gave their lives to Christ that week. Oh, how I wished I could feel the security of my salvation and the prayer I had prayed, so that week I also went forward and rededicated my life to Christ. Surely, I thought, this time I would feel salvation had actually taken place for me. To walk the aisle again and go through the baptismal waters again would surely bring me to the closeness of Christ I so desperately longed to have.

But time passed, and I was still plagued with the dreams of Satan's demons being after me. Night after night I woke, knowing I was doomed to Hell. So I began praying the prayer of salvation over and over. Surely if I said it enough times, one of those prayers would get me the peace in my heart I needed. I went to every church service, every church camp I could afford, and every youth retreat open to me. Hopefully I would hear something somewhere that would assure me I most certainly was saved.

The summer of my sophomore/junior year I spent time away from home as much as possible. My bff Rachel and I were on the road constantly, attending as many revivals and church services as we could. Again, I felt drawn to God with every invitation, so I went forward almost every time. Everyone thought I was already a Christian, so I went forward to pray, so they believed. But mostly when I was kneeling, I just cried. I didn't know why I was there or what I was longing for. I had already prayed the sinners' prayer so many times, surely by now I was saved. So I just knelt there crying.

Eventually I decided that because I must be saved, God was calling me to be more for Him, that He must be calling me to become a missionary. The first one I told was my mother. How proud she was! It was the first time in my life I felt like she was happy with me and the choices I made. This brought a closeness we had never had before, and that contentment only reassured me I had made the right decision. I then went to my pastor and he did some research and found a program called Sojourners. It was a ministry of the Southern Baptist Convention for kids between their Junior and Senior years who felt they were being called into the ministry. They would spend the summer away from home getting their feet wet as a missionary.

I couldn't wait for the paperwork to come, so I could reserve my space. When it arrived, I was almost overwhelmed with all the forms and questions I had to fill out. My church had said they would donate some of the money I needed for the summer away, and I would start saving some on my own that I made from mowing and babysitting so I would have enough. I worked hard getting all the forms turned in by the January deadline. How excited I was to follow what I felt like was my destiny.

But as is such with anyone who sets their hearts to do something amazing for God, Satan set in to attempt to make me fall. He sent into my life who I thought was my true love. A young man a few years older than I, tall, blue eyed and drove a cool car. We ended up spending way too much time alone and my heart was pulled to that love too much. How guilty I felt that I was about to embark on my most important journey ever, and here I was allowing sin to run rampant in my life. In my head and heart, I knew I needed to get right with God before I left, so I broke up with him a few weeks before the trip. He was terribly hurt but we both promised we would just take the summer to decide what was best for us and we would get back together when I returned.

I left early in June and was sent to a Mission Center in a neighboring state. It was right in the heart of a big city, something this country girl knew nothing about. There were about twenty girls and 15 boys. Five of us were still in high school, the rest were part of another missionary program for college students. We spent the summer holding vacation bible schools each weekday morning for kids, and spending the evenings giving out food and clothing. There was also one evening each week when a doctor would come in and see to the people's medical needs. It was a wonderful ministry, and I loved every part of it. I also made great friends, some of which I am still friends with today.

In the evenings, the mission was open to the teenagers in the community. There was a gymnasium where we spent a lot of time playing basketball and volleyball. After I had been there about a week, I was on teen ministry duty. That job consisted of just mingling with the local teens, getting to know them and building relationships in order to share Jesus with them. I was very athletic, and so I was setting on the stage in the gym watching the guys play ball, wishing they would ask me to join in. There was a boy there who I had not seen before and we had was an instant attraction. It was one of those that pull you in so fast you don't know what's happening.

I couldn't take my eyes off of him, but romantic relationships between the local boys and girls were strictly forbidden. I had to get out of there, so I left and went into the kitchen area just to get away and pull my thoughts and feelings back together. I had never felt so close to someone I had never even met, and as I stood there trying to figure out what was happening, he came in behind me. Oh, how handsome he was, and Lee and I had an instant connection.

Several times over the next few weeks we were reprimanded for flirting and talking, so we began to sneak with our communications. First it was late night phone calls, but we were caught, so we then began meeting outside after dark. Caught again, we resorted to means that can only be trouble for young teens who aren't allowed to talk. Needless to say, I went home pregnant. He was Hispanic and in my small town the only Hispanics I had known were the ones who came in for a couple months each year to pick apples. I knew what that meant to my mother and my church; how embarrassed and ashamed they would be at what I had done.

He had asked me to marry him, and I said yes in hopes that this bond would keep us tied together for the following year until I could graduate high school and return to him. Now that a baby was involved and I would be facing the shame of what I had done, I had to make new plans. I decided I would keep the baby hidden until Christmas because by then I would have enough credits to receive my diploma. The only thing I would miss would be graduating with my classmates I had spent so many years with. But to stay there and face the shame I had brought, would be more than I could bear.

We had written many letters in the month after I returned home, and I had told him I was pretty sure I was pregnant and also of my plans to come back to him at Christmas time. He had replied and in his letter, he asked me if I had found out for sure yet. I had to continue life as normal in order to keep my plan in place. That week I had volleyball camp and was spending every day for several hours at school, and I had left that letter laying on my night stand in my bedroom. My parents were pretty respectful of my privacy and to my knowledge had never nosed or pried into anything in my room before. It never came to mind that I should put it away.

Later that evening, after I went to bed and my mother had gotten in the shower, my dad came and got me out of bed and took me into the kitchen for a talk. He had never done this before and I had a feeling I knew what was coming. That day, while I was gone, he had seen the letter laying there. He told me he had never done anything like that before but something told him to pick up that letter and read it. He asked me if I was pregnant, and I told him I didn't know for sure but I was fairly positive. He wanted to know what happened and how much in love with the father I was, so it all came flooding out. It felt good to let it out and tell the truth. I didn't feel alone now and my dad's sincere concern for me was something new I had never felt from him before.

My mother eventually got out of the shower and came in and sat down at the table with us. We were both quiet for a few moments and then my dad spoke up, and she realized what was going on. She began to cry and asked me over and over how I could do this to her. There it was, the shame I knew she would feel. All I could do was cry and my father soon shut her down. He could see the pain that I was feeling at shaming, her and he couldn't take it. He also could see how much I loved Lee because I was willing to leave everything I had or had ever known to be with him. He told me he would call him and tell Lee that if he would come there and marry me, he would help us get started in life by providing us a place to live and helping him to get a job.

At that my mother, enraged, stood up and slammed her hand on the table and stated that she would NOT have a Mexican living in her home. My dad quickly told her he would not have his grandchild grow up without a father and blame him for it. That if we didn't get married, it would be by Lee's choice and not his. My mother sat back down, and I could feel the heat of anger emanating from her.

I don't remember much more about that night other than a lot of crying. The mixture of emotions was beyond anything I had ever felt. Since I was a little girl, being a mother was all I ever wanted. To do it this way was not in my plan, but I knew God was the giver of the child, and He had given me this life inside. Now that my parents knew what I had done, I never wanted anything more. Even though I had shamed them and was about to shame many others in my church, all I wanted was this child. I wanted him to be safe and happy and healthy. I would never love anything or anyone more than the love I felt that night. I would do whatever I needed to protect and care for him.

First a home test, and then a doctor's visit both confirmed what I already knew. I wrote to Lee the next day and told him all that had transpired. I told him my dad was going to call him and what he was going to say. A couple weeks later on the phone my dad spoke to him very kindly and told him just what he had promised me he would. The next few weeks were agonizing for me. I hadn't heard from him so I went to my friend's house and called him collect. He told me he was coming and that his parents were trying to find a time they could bring him.

But no more letters came and the next time I tried to call, his phone had been shut off. How the real hurt began to set in! Many of my friends turned their backs on me, and I never felt so alone. My mother wouldn't speak to me at all and most of the adults at church wouldn't even look my way. One evening I was trying to decide on a name and had written some down on a piece of paper. I left the paper on the kitchen table and when I woke the next morning I was told by her she was not ready for that, and I was not to do it again. If I did, I was not to leave it where she could see it.

Since we were living back in the country I had a lot of time to walk that winter. My mother kept telling me it was the best way to stay healthy through the pregnancy, and my doctor kept reminding me not to gain too much weight, or I would not lose it all. There were several cliffs in the woods where I lived and more than once I found myself standing at the tops of those cliffs, wishing someone would come along and give me a shove and the loneliness I felt would be over. But I had no desire to hurt my child, I had always wanted a child and to be a mother, and I was now his protector, and I was grateful, so grateful for him.

Months went by and I didn't hear from Lee until I was in my third trimester. I had been going to the mail box every day, hoping he would realize how close I was getting and would be telling me when he would be there. Then one day when I came home from school, there was a letter lying on my pillow. The envelope was all scrunched up and looked like it had been opened. I asked my mother if she had opened it, only to be met with a quick and short no. It was different than his other letters in that it was only one paragraph, where the others had been two or three pages each. It said he was seeing someone else now and that he would be moving soon and would send money for the baby.

What a fool I had been to believe he really loved me. How could I fall so quickly for someone I hardly knew and to give him my heart so completely? I sat down immediately and wrote back to him that I didn't want any of his money and to just leave me and my baby alone. The anger set in and I curled into myself and decided I would never let him into my heart again. From that point on I had given up on his love and, so I thought, he had given up on loving me. It would be years later before I would learn the truth of why he didn't come, but my heart told me that someday he would find the person he would truly love and I was somehow ok with that. I was going to trust God to take care of me and my child, and I was trusting Lee would also find happiness.

True Love Always Hopes

Jerusalem, Jerusalem, you who kill the prophets and
stone those sent to you, how often I have longed to
gather your children together, as a hen gathers her
chicks under her wings, and you were not willing.
Matthew 23:37

Jerusalem first appears in the Bible in Genesis as the city of Salem where Melchizedek was king. Its next appearance is in Joshua 10:1 when the king was trying to make a plan to defeat Joshua as he led the Israelites through the land God had promised them, conquering as they went. It later became known as the City of David, after David settled there and made it the capital. His son Solomon then built the temple there and hailed it "a place for You to dwell forever." 1 Kings 8:13.

The old testament goes on to tell us of the sin of the kings that ruled there and how they kept worshiping and encouraging the people worship other god's, something the Lord had strictly forbidden many years before. God then allowed other nations to come and war against and rule over the Israelites until they decided they were done with their sin, turning back to God who would then come to their rescue and allow them to live in peace again. For years all God wanted for them was to be true to Him, not worshipping other gods. He had been the One to care for them and give them the land, but over and over their hearts continued to go astray.

Jesus was addressing this problem in this verse in Matthew. He was saying to them that for so long all God wanted was to care for them, like a hen cares for her chicks. But they had kept running out from under His sheltering wing with their sin, where He couldn't protect them anymore. God now made a way for their sin to be forgiven when He sent Jesus to be the final sin sacrifice. Now all they would need to do was to believe that Jesus was the promised Messiah, but the Pharisees and the teachers of the law were still unbelieving. It had been Jesus's hope, and still is His hope, that all would believe in Him so we can all get to heaven. John 3:16 For God so loved the world that He gave His only begotten Son, that who-soever believes in Him should not perish, but have everlasting life.

Stefan was born just before I graduated in the spring of my senior year. Soon after, I began dating a young man I had known for a few years and three months later we married. My mother and I were fighting so bad then, I was willing to do whatever I had to in order to move out. I had tried to rent a low-income apartment, but since I had not had a job long enough, they wouldn't let me have one. The marriage was difficult and after the birth of my second son, it only got worse. Our differences greatly outweighed any liking we had for each other in the beginning, and just short of five years later, we were signing divorce papers.

But even before the marriage was over, I was already on the look-out for another true love. I knew there had to be someone out there for me who could love me for who I was. It wasn't long before God found him for me. I was selling a popular skin care line and was in the same unit with his sister-in-law. One day I was complaining about all the dates I had been on and she asked me what kind of man

I was looking for. After telling her my list, she suggested I date her brother-in-law. A week later we met at her house on a blind date. It was the first blind date I had ever been on, and it was also the last.

Twenty-eight days went by and we were saying I do. Roger had never been married before and had no children of his own so an instant family was a new thing for him, and it was hard for me to allow him to be the dad he wanted to be. But he loved kids, and loving my two sons was easy for him and he has been the best father anyone could ever ask for. I was very happy with the choice I had made to marry him and we truly were living happily ever after. Oh, our marriage has not been perfect, as no marriage is, but I believe it to be the very best marriage anyone could have.

Almost two years later, when I was six months pregnant with our daughter, we had a revival at our church and the evangelist said to us, to me, "If you have lived all your life, wondering if you were saved, that's not the devil making you doubt, it's the Holy Spirit telling you that you need to be saved." There was my answer I had been searching for so long. I had talked to different pastors about my doubts and they all told me the same thing, if I had prayed the prayer, then I was saved. But this evangelist went on to tell me that, "It's like when you sit on a chair, you believe the chair will hold you up, but until you sit on it, you don't have faith that it will." That's what I had been doing. I had believed in Jesus because I had known about Him all my life, but I had never put my faith in his promise that when I asked Him to save me, he would.

That night I went home and cried all night long, not because I wasn't saved, but because I finally knew what I had been doing wrong all these years. The next morning early, Roger took me back to the church and I prayed the sinners' prayer for the last time there in the pastor's office. I have never since doubted my salvation and am so grateful for the work God began in me that day.

As all marriages go, life settled in and I began once again to wonder if I had made a mistake. When you only date someone for twenty-eight days you don't really know them or who they are, and so you have to learn as you go. I was young and learning, and many times felt insecure in his love. I had been given a book called Love Life and had never read it. It was about Christian marriage and what you must do to maintain it. Inside it told me that to have a true love with my spouse, I needed to let go of all other previous loves I had ever had. At the moment I read that, something I was not willing to do, I put the book down and didn't pick it up again for years.

After the birth of our fourth child, I was really struggling with my own insecurity and what I had been through. My dad had died, and I was so torn in my feelings about his death so I began counseling. I just opened the phone book and called the first Christian counselor I found. When I arrived in his office, it happened to be in a building that had been named after the author of the book I had put down years earlier. He had originally owned that building and counseled out of it for some time. I had no idea about this when I made that call, and I knew then God had once again worked this out for me.

I met with him several times over that year, and he helped me work through my feelings of my past and how God had taken care of me and kept my "head above water." He helped me see that life and love are about more than me and my insecurity and my search to be loved. He helped me see that Roger's love for me could never be enough to fill the longing that only the true love of Christ could fill. He helped me see that Roger's love for me, as small as an act could be, is still love, and I truly was in the best place I could be.

Here we are, twenty-three years, five children, three grandchildren, two daughters-in-law, and one son-in-law later, and I still find my insecurity that Roger truly loves me to be a problem when I try to make him be the fulfiller of my emptiness. Even with the hand-written love notes at the top of the comic pages every day, the random cherry limeades, the flowers and the dates, I still sometimes feel the need to continue to look for a love I have already found. But when I focus my looking on the love Christ has given, then that longing leaves me and I can put my hope in His love and let it fill my emptiness.

True Love is Perseverant

For you know that God paid a ransom to save you from the
empty life you inherited from your ancestors. And it was not
paid with mere gold or silver, which lose their value. It was the
precious blood of Christ, the sinless, spotless Lamb of God.
1 Peter 1:18-19

What empty life is Peter talking about here? He is referring to
the laws that God laid down at the beginning. All the rules
and regulations the people needed to keep in order to be counted
righteous before God were nothing but emptiness and a burden. So
why did God create all these laws and rules in the first place? Clearly,
we as sinful humans can't keep them all every day of our lives, so what
good did they do? They were created to show us we are not perfect and
we can't get to God by our own works. We must have Someone else to
do it for us, we must have a Savior to keep these rules and laws for us.

Peter also tells us we aren't getting to heaven by buying our way
in. Some religions will teach you the more you have the closer to God
you must be, therefore it's your duty to give more and more to the
church in order to pay for the sin you have committed. Bologna!!!
Jesus never taught that we need to amass riches or we needed to give
our riches to receive forgiveness. In fact, He told us we need to leave
what we have, take up our cross, and follow Him. How do we do
that? By doing our best (and our best isn't going to be perfect so stop

trying) each day. And when our best has been less than perfect, then we ask God's forgiveness and try again.

The ransom paid for us was the blood Jesus shed on the cross. In the empty life that had been inherited from their ancestors, the people were required to offer different sacrifices for different sins. So when Jesus came along, and lived sinless for us, He became our perfect sacrifice, and if we believe in Him and what He did for us, then His blood covers all sin. In Hebrews 10:14 we are told, "For by one sacrifice He has made perfect forever those who are being made holy."

Jesus made us perfect forever! Does this mean once we accept Him as our Savior our life will be perfect from then on out? No! In fact, the Christian life is hard and difficult. It's easier to do whatever you want whenever you want than to walk a life pleasing to Him. It's easier to be whatever the world says you can or should be than to deny ourselves and take up our cross and follow Him. It's easier to find our lives than to lose them for His sake. But if we have put our faith and trust in Jesus to take care of us and help us through this difficult walk of life, then our perfection is not in who we are, but in who He is and we can throw down that burden and live free and happy in who He has created us to be.

This is the goal of His perseverant love for us. John 15:9-12 "As the Father has loved me, so I have loved you. Now remain in my love. If you keep my commands, you will remain in my love, just as I have kept my Father's commands and remain in His love. I have told you this so that my joy may be in you and that your joy may be ·complete. My command is this; that you love each other as I have loved you." And how did He love us? Perseveringly, "even unto death on the cross." Phillipians 2:8

Our daughter Sarah had graduated with her associates degree and decided she was ready for the world. Her boyfriend would be playing football in college, and she had fallen for the city life dearly. Every time she went to the same big city I had spent that summer in so many years before, she felt more and more drawn there. So as soon as she could, she packed her things and headed that way. She had found an apartment and only gathered a few things for it when I loaded up the van with all I could and went to see her new home.

I had only been back there a handful of times since that summer twenty-eight years ago, and every time I was nervous and scared I would see Lee. I always worried how I would feel and react. Would he even remember me or that I had borne his child? When I got to Sarah's, her boyfriend told us his dad wanted to take us out to eat that night, so we headed into the city. As we got close, that scared, nervous feeling arose in me again. Closer and closer we came to where I had spent that summer and when he took the exit the old mission center was on, scared and nervous turned to anxiousness. He came to the light, the very light I had been through so many times before, and I told him to turn left.

Immediately we came upon the mission center and as I looked at it the anxiety turned to love and excitement as the memories of all that had happened there flooded my mind. The vacation bible schools, the medical clinics, the clothing distributions, the wonderful friends, it all came back so quickly that I was overwhelmed. Then, as expected, Lee filled my mind and I remembered that sometimes he went by a nickname. I had searched for him only a few times on social media over the years, and had actually seen his picture without realizing it. I don't know why this memory hadn't hit me before, so the next morning when I searched for the nickname, there he was!

He looked nothing like what I had remembered and I wouldn't have known it was him if it weren't for an old school picture he had posted too. Should I write to him? Should I even try to re-establish contact after all these years? How had he been? Had he lived happily ever after like I hoped he did? Did Stefan have any siblings and if he did, how many? Were there any medical issues he had that Stefan should be concerned about or watch for? All these questions filled my mind as, hands shaking, I was able to type out a message to him asking if he were the same Lee I had known so long ago. The next morning, he answered and said yes, it was him, and his excitement at my finding him was evident.

We talked about Stefan and I sent him a few pictures, so he could see him and know that he was doing good. He had never even known I had a boy because he hadn't received the pictures I sent him a few months after Stefan was born. I tried to keep my information about our son at a minimum because I didn't know how Stefan would feel at my being in contact with Lee again. Stefan had expressed a desire to know him several years earlier, but we hadn't talked about it in a while, and I didn't know he had already made peace with possibly not ever meeting him.

But Lee told me that first week that he had always loved me, and he had always known I was the one he should have lived his life with. So I asked him why didn't he come when my dad called him. He said it was because his letters were returned to him, along with a letter from my parents telling him they were sending me away until after the baby was born. That he couldn't come because he was Hispanic and they were going to raise the baby themselves. He said he had kept the letters in hopes that if we ever came back into his life he could show us why he didn't come, but unfortunately, they had burned in a house fire. He also said he had never written to me again because he didn't want to cause any more trouble for me than he already had, so the letter that came in the Spring I thought was from him, wasn't.

I was certain he was lying and I showed the messages to Roger and told him I was sure it was all a lie. But Lee kept saying it was true, and with each new detail as I probed deeper into the possibility, he kept to his story and it didn't change. So I called my mother, one of the few times we had been on speaking terms through the years, and this conversation took place.

"It doesn't matter to me after all these years, I am happy in my life and I have no intentions on going anywhere, but I really need to know the truth. Did you send Lee's letters back to him and send him a letter yourself telling him not to come?"

She immediately blurted out, "No."

"Well, he says you did." I replied.

"Are you speaking to him?" she asked.

I answered, "Yes, I found him online and he says that you sent his letters back and sent him one too, telling him not to come."

Only silence came from the other end of the phone, and as I gave her the chance to remember and reflect, she said, "Dad and I just always believed that if he loved you the way he said he did, then he would have been here."

We went on to talk some more about other things and the conversation ended on what I thought was a good note, but when I tried to reach her a few more times later on, she didn't answer or return my messages. About a month went by before the memories of that time came back to me because the pain had been too much, and I had blocked many of them out. But as each one trickled in, I began to realize his story was true, and as I asked more and more questions that he was able to supply answers to, it all began to make sense to me. It was the answer to why my mother had acted and spoke the way she did toward me during and after the pregnancy. It was the answer to why she treated Stefan so well after he was born even though he himself was also Hispanic. And it was the answer to why I had always felt like there was more to my life's story.

When the reality of it finally set in, I was lying in bed crying when Roger came in and sat down beside me, as he does before he leaves for work on a regular basis. I poured all my anger and hurt out to him and he sat quietly listening. I was scared at how he would feel, but I needed to tell him what was going on. I asked him then what he thought about it all, afraid that he would be upset I had even contacted Lee again in the first place, but he had only compassion for me. He understood totally my tears; I was so grateful for a husband who wasn't screaming at me for even thinking about contacting a past love.

The next several months were, I can honestly say, the most difficult I have ever experienced. I had nothing but disdain for the birthday card that came from my mother and when a Christmas card came along later, feelings weren't any better. Stefan and Lee had started texting and talking a little bit and it made me happy they could at least be able to talk and know how each other were doing. But Lee had not lived happily ever after; he had lived a very difficult life full of decisions that had only caused him more pain. This revelation only added to my anger at my mother and my feeling that if he had been with me, I would have never allowed him to make those bad choices and everything would have been okay for him.

These feelings were magnified when I saw him one day. Stefan and I had gone down to watch a football game at the college Sarah's boyfriend attended. The fair was in town and I had told Lee we might go. He showed up there and walked around until he found us. He walked right up to Stefan, shook his hand and said hello. When I turned to see them talking, a numbness took over me and I didn't even know what to say or how to feel. There they were, father and son, talking for the first time and I felt like the world stopped. They talked for a few minutes and he said hello to me too and then went on his way.

Back to the counselor for me it was! I told him my sob story, my best yet he had said, and I tried to explain the mixed feelings invading my heart and mind. He told me I was a fixer, and these feelings were coming from my need to make everything okay. He also reminded me I have a great capacity to love, and the fact that I was so torn about this was not out of character for me. But he asked me a question I had not ever had to answer before which began the healing process for me. He asked me who I was!

I had not really thought about it, and I immediately came back with the answer that as a Christian was the right thing to say, "I am a

Christian!" I replied. "But that doesn't tell me who you are," he said. So before my next visit I had to think about and figure out who I was and what my purpose in life was. To do that, I had to take myself back to my childhood and what the desires of my heart had been, before all the bad, before all the anger and heartache. I knew from the time I was small my greatest desire was to be a mother. The dolls and stuffed animals and pets and little brother, I had been a mother to them all and I couldn't wait to grow up and become a real mother.

I also knew that I was a wife. Along with the dream of being a mother, came the desire to be a good wife to the man of my dreams. I had actually dreamed about Roger once, before I ever met him. After we married, I was able to share that dream with him, which actually came true at the birth of Sarah. Being a great wife meant the world to me as a child, and I couldn't wait to meet my future husband, hence the constant searching. Then lastly, I knew I was a Christian. I had known since the last time I had prayed to receive Christ that my salvation was assured then and had never doubted again.

Lee and I had a very difficult time for a while getting along, a friendship was hard to develop after all that had happened and how different our worlds were, but we tried and fought several times. The last time was mostly my fault. I had tried to step in and help him out when he hadn't asked me to, and when it didn't work out like I thought it would, I had to share what I had done with Roger and he had the perfect solution to the problem. I felt bad I had not told him about it in the first place. A few weeks later, as we lay in bed at night and I was so upset at the whole thing, he snuggled up next to me and held me as I cried. I cried because of my anger at my mother for causing all this to happen. I cried because Lee had not lived happily ever after like I had hoped. And I cried because I had a husband who was so understanding that he would hold his wife as she cried over another man.

Since then, Lee and I have found a balance in our new friendship and I am content that he is living the life he wants. My counselor told me I could run away and chase after the past, but that story was written every day and more often than not, it never works out because people soon realize why they parted in the first place. He told me not to let that be the story I wrote, and that statement has helped me to keep my eye on the prize, the prize of being the best mother, wife, and Christian I can be. Roger's perseverant love for me has been what has kept me on this path God has put me on, the reason I have been able to "run the race that has been set before me." Hebrews 12:1

True Love Never Fails

Later, knowing that everything had now been finished, and
so that Scripture would be fulfilled, Jesus said, "I am thirsty."
A jar of wine vinegar was there, so they soaked a sponge in it,
put the sponge on a stalk of the hyssop plant, and lifted it to
Jesus's lips. When He had received the drink, Jesus said, "It is
finished." With that, He bowed His head and gave up the Spirit.
John 19:28-30

This chapter is the most difficult for me to write because every
time I think of Jesus dying for my sin on that cross I get sick-
ness and sadness in my stomach. I hate He had to do that for me,
yet He did it willingly. I know I have stated over and over He lived
sinless for us, but I just don't think we realize, as people, how difficult a task that was. Have you ever tried to live just one day without
sinning? I know it would have been impossible for me, but Jesus told
us over and over He and the Father were one, so He knew His task
from the very beginning and saw it through all the way to the end.

He could have stopped it long before it came to the end on the
cross. He could have chosen what part He wanted to do and what
part He didn't want to do. "Um, ok, I will take the being made fun
of, but I don't want anyone to spit on me. And a simple whipping will
be ok, but don't let them use the one with the glass and rocks tied to
it. And you can let them put a crown of thorns on me but make sure

the briars aren't too long so they don't go too far into my scalp." But he didn't say these things, instead He went all the way and He took whatever man chose to do to Him. He didn't cry out for help or try to defend Himself. He took it all! By finishing what He set out to do, He showed His love for us truly was and always will be unfailing.

My son Samuel began dating Faye his senior year of high school. She was a quiet and shy young girl and very pretty. He brought her to the house a few times and I instantly loved her. She was always willing to help out whenever she could and she was easy for me to talk to. When it was prom time and I had to buy her dress, she was so thankful and expressed her gratitude to me over and over. But Faye lived in a terrible world of abuse and disease. Her mother had died of Huntington's disease, and she and her younger brother were being tested for it too.

The tests both came back positive and her brother was not expected to make it through high school, but Faye's was a slower growing kind and her life expectancy was early fifties. Just after high school, she and Samuel broke up, and she moved in with a young man named John. They were never married but had one child, Jeremiah. As her disease progressed, much faster than the doctor had predicted, she and John began to have problems, and she became increasingly difficult for anyone to get along with.

Eventually, Faye and Jeremiah ended up at the Salvation Army, but when her time there was almost up, and they would be forced to live on the streets, I brought them home with me. I had no idea how bad her Huntington's had progressed, and they were not here long before I realized that living in my home, with my own children and my stairs, was not going to work for her at all. Once we were able to get her SSI started, I, along with my friends and church family, moved them into an apartment in town.

I continued to take care of them though and soon saw her disease had progressed beyond being able to continue to adequately care for a four-year-old son. John was there as much as he could be and took Jeremiah to pre-school every morning, but he still couldn't deal with her mood swings and bullying tactics to get her way. John also was not in a position at that time to properly care for Jeremiah, so after about six months, someone called DHS on her and they were able to gather enough information to put Jeremiah in a foster home.

Eventually, John and his new wife were able to get custody of Jeremiah and I was hopeful John would be able to be the dad that Jeremiah needed him to be. However, John struggled with depression and drinking and one night in a drunken state, he picked up a gun and shot himself. He lived for a few months before an infection settled in his brain, took over, and John died. John's dad and stepmom then filed for guardianship of Jeremiah as Faye's health had continued to decline.

They then called me and asked if I would tell the judge what I knew about Faye's condition and inability to properly care for Jeremiah. I told them I would, as long as she was not present in the room. She had moved in with her new boyfriend and his mother, but I wanted to be able to continue to care for her if someday it ever came to that again. Later that evening, while talking to their attorney, he asked me if I thought Faye would object to Jeremiah living with his grandparents and I said yes. When he asked why, I told him she was his mother and always had been. She may forget who she is someday, but she will always remember he is her son. The love of a mother is an unfailing love that no matter the disease, will never be something in her that will die.

As I look back and reflect on the times in my own life that love has not failed me, there are several instances I can fall back on. At the lake when I kept bobbing up and down in the water, I know God was there, holding me up and giving me the strength to keep going until my mother saw me. I know it was God that had given

Luke the knowledge to unplug that extension cord when he heard my voice crying his name. I know when that dog was attacking me and biting my face. it was God that allowed me to get my feet under his stomach just right and shove him away. As I stood there holding my mother's bottle of pills, I know it was God that had made my dad believe what he did about suicide so I wouldn't swallow them all. And as I stood at the top of those cliffs wanting to jump, I know it was God that had given the child inside of me to keep me here to accomplish His good works in me.

Now, as I live day by day, I know it is God that has blessed me so abundantly in my life by giving me five amazing children, their spouses and children, and a husband who loves me with an unfailing, perseverant love. I know I have many friends and family that love me with this same unfailing love. And I know that when I look to Jesus to fill the void of love that man leaves behind, His love is more unfailing than anything I have ever dreamed love is.

What is True Love?

Whoever has my commands and keeps them is the one
who loves me. The one who loves me, will be loved by my
Father, and I too will love them and show myself to them.
John 14:21

Jesus's greatest desire after His work was finished is that we would believe in Him and who He was and His message. He gave us many commands in His time here and that would be a subject for a whole different book I myself am not qualified to write, but for someone who has dug into and researched the Bible much more than me. But one command I do know, that He wants us to love Him and to love God and to love each other.

So what is true love? True love is all of the things that 1 Corinthians 13 tells us it is. True love is the actions of being patient, kind, not envious, not boastful, not proud, not rude, not self-seeking, not easily angered, keeping no record of wrongs, not delighting in evil but rejoicing in the truth, protecting, trusting, persevering, and never failing. We aren't going to show every one of these attributes all the time to everyone we meet, but when we do show them individually and to anyone at all, we are giving true love.

But I want to add here one more attribute that I believe Jesus showed as His life produced each of these actions of love. He did them unexpectant! When He did each of these things in His life,

He never asked anyone for anything in return. He did everything He did simply because He loves us and wants us to be with Him someday. When we show these actions of love to others, and we expect nothing in return, then we are giving true love. When these things are done for us, and there is nothing expected from us in return, we have been truly loved. It doesn't have to be only from a spouse or a child or a family member or friend, it can be from or for a total stranger.

And even as I have been writing these words to you, I have still been learning what love is and isn't. When I give love, and I expect that love in return, it isn't true love. Even if all I get from it is the feeling I have done something good, then my love has not been true. And these past few months, as I have changed the way I have given love, something wonderful has happened. I am no longer hurt or disappointed when that love isn't returned when or like I thought it should be, and that unexpectant love has freed me to be loved the way others love, not the way I want or expect to be loved.

I know my grandmother loved me because of the kindness that she always showed. I know Lindsey loved me and I love her despite my envy of the wonderful things she had, and I wish we lived closer so that our friendship could continue like it was when we were kids. I know despite our disagreements, Luke will always want to protect and love me and I will always love him. I am still as proud to be Tom's big sister as I was back then, and I hope he knows how much I truly love him. I know my mother has done the best she can, for the circumstances given her, and that whether what she did to Lee and I was wrong or right, she is my mother and a mother's love never dies. My dad did all he could for me during my pregnancy to show His unselfish love by being understanding and reaching out to my heart in ways I never knew he could.

My aunt Susan still shows her love to me every time I see her or talk to her just through the excitement in her voice at my visits. Mine and Kate's love has been through some difficult times, but has grown stronger with each battle and I know it always will be true. As a mother and teacher of children I have discovered that the truth of an event usually falls somewhere between both sides of the story. Since finding him again, Lee and I have had a very difficult friendship, but I am still trusting God to take care of him and to give him His happily ever after. I've never felt like I deserve the love Roger has shown for me over the years, but I know it is the true love that I spent so long hoping for. In court Faye was able to tell the Judge how bad her disease had progressed herself, so my testimony was not needed, but no matter how much it continues to steal her mind and her body, her unfailing love for her son will never disappear from her heart. Jesus, well what more can I say about His love but this, "This is how we know what love is; Jesus Christ laid down His life for us." 1 John 3:16.

As for the family member I spoke about at the beginning of this book, the one who tested my love to the fullest, we have since spoken once. He did what I asked him to so my hurt can begin to heal and forgiveness can take root, instead of anger and disappointment. I don't believe I ever stopped loving him, or I wouldn't have been so hurt in the first place. His actions afterward would not have been something I dwelt on for so long if I had stopped loving him. And even if he had not done what I asked, it still would have been a requirement of me, as a follower of Christ, to forgive him and continue loving him, the same way Christ continues to love and forgive me.

I have no idea what your love story is or the journey of love you have been on, but no matter your story, please know this, Jesus is the answer to your story, just as he has been mine. Man is not perfect, never has been and never will be, and when we look to man to fill the longing for true love that each of us are born with, we will become disappointed over and over again. Jesus's one goal was to make a way for us to be with Him eternally. All we need to do to fulfill His goal, is accept His perfect gift of salvation.

The Sinners Prayer of Salvation

Father God,

I know that I am a sinner. I believe that Jesus was your one and only Son that you sent to die on the cross for my sins and that He now lives in Heaven with you. Please forgive me of those sins. I give my life to you. Work in my life and help me to be the Christ follower that you want me to be.

In Jesus's Name, I Pray.
Amen

If you pray this prayer, please get a Bible as soon as you can and begin reading it. I like to tell people to start with the gospels, Matthew, Mark, Luke and John. I prefer to read the New International Version of the Bible. I am not a big word's kind of person and it's easy for me to understand. Then, if it is a possibility, find a local, Bible believing church and begin going on a regular basis. This will help you to continue to grow in your new faith and immerse yourself into a new family that will truly love you with all their hearts. Thank you for reading this book to the end and I pray that you will find that Jesus will fill those empty spaces in your heart like no man can.

Bibliography

Bible. (2016). *The Bible, NIV Version.* You Version.

Commentary, N.-M. 1. (1985). *Holy Bible New International Verson.* Grand Rapids, MI: The Zondervan Corporation.

Dexter, H. (2017). *Jewish Belief that the Spirit Lingers for Three Days.* Retrieved from peopleof.oureverydaylife.com: www.peopleof. oureverydaylife.com

Evie. (1977). Four Feet Eleven. *Mirror.*

Google Dictionary. (n.d.).

Printed in the United States
By Bookmasters